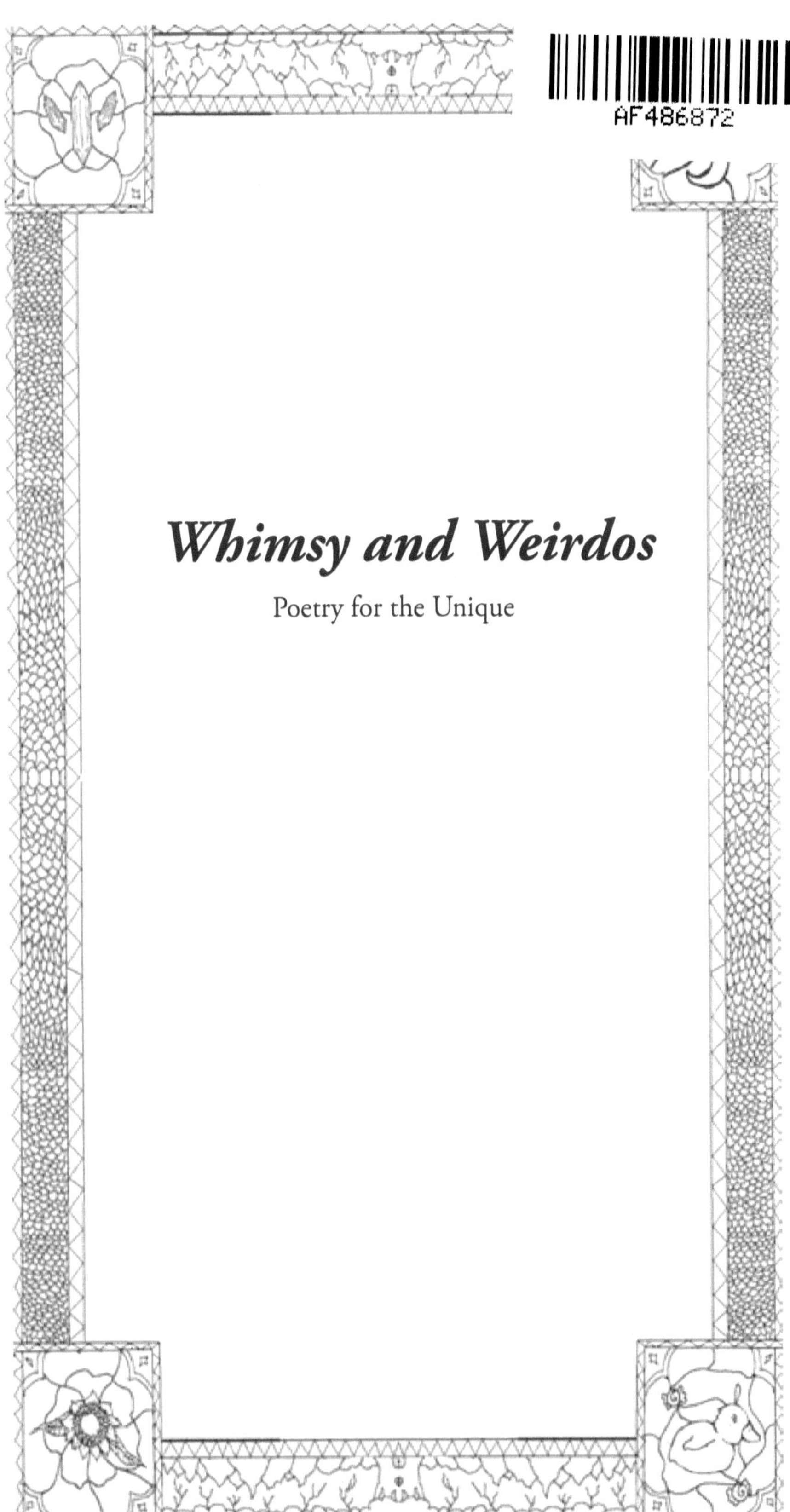

Whimsy and Weirdos

Poetry for the Unique

Also by

Andrea Standifer
Gracie the Clinic Cat
Through Riley's Eyes

Machelle Berglund
Through the Shards of My
Heart

Table of Contents

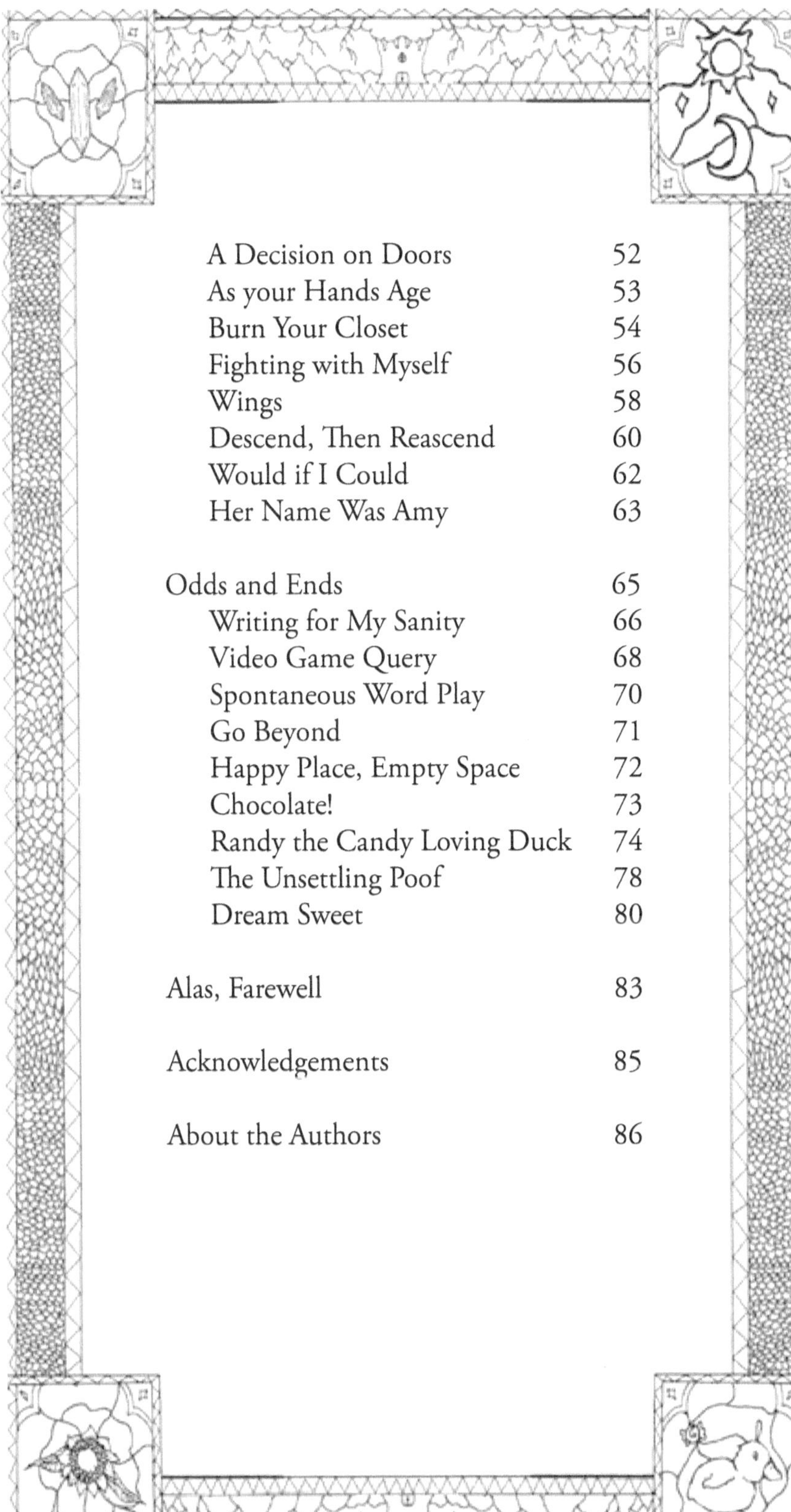

A Little Welcoming Poem

When the day is long,
bullies you all throughout,
makes you feel a stranger
to the world of the human
race,
and you need someplace to
go,
a place that takes you as you
are,
doesn't ask you to change,
then I know a place you can
go;
Its right between these
pages,
within the ink,
scrawled onto paper by a
writer's hand

The guardian of this text,
the page master,
stands before the gateway
with a friendly face
and kindly gestures,
proudly proclaiming
to all who listen;

"Come one, come all!
Welcome weirdos!
Welcome whimscy-ists!
Welcome everyone and all!
This tome was meant for
you
So turn the page,
take a gander,
get cozy and stay awhile"

"Everyone has a weirdo
within
why not let them out
and have a little fun?
Let the words dance
within the jelly of your
brain,
their meaning washing over
you
like a cleansing rain"

"This life won't last forever,
but sometimes you need a
break
from the stresses of the day
to day,
to feel a little something
more,
to feel a little sorrow,
to feel a little joy,
to feel a kinship with others
you may have never felt
before"

"And so my fellow weirdos,
and my freaky friends,
I hope you find this
to be within your heart's
delight,
and from here,
we will start-"

"Turn the page and-
Ready.
Set.

Go!"

The Whimsy of Imagination

Poems of Fantasy

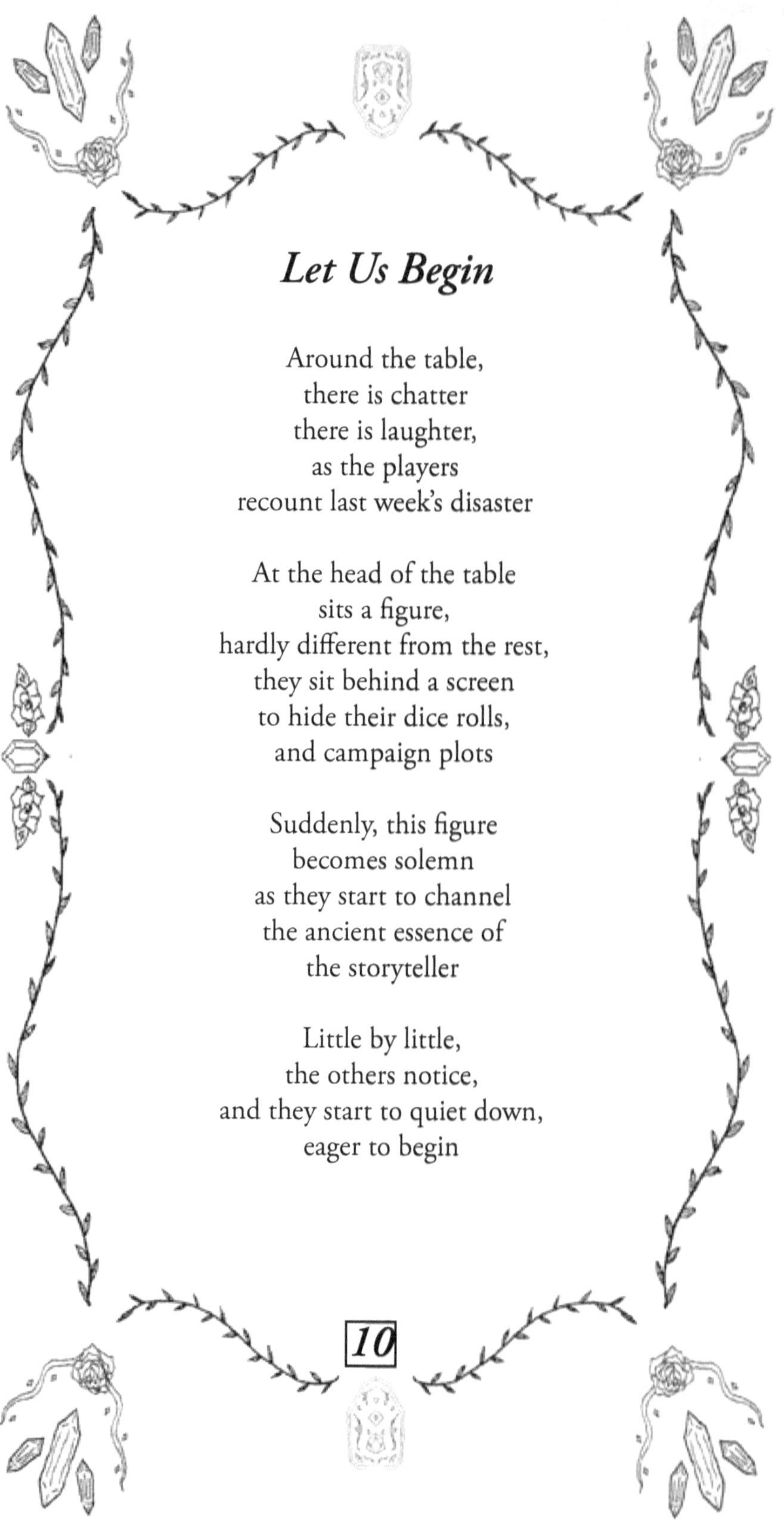

Let Us Begin

Around the table,
there is chatter
there is laughter,
as the players
recount last week's disaster

At the head of the table
sits a figure,
hardly different from the rest,
they sit behind a screen
to hide their dice rolls,
and campaign plots

Suddenly, this figure
becomes solemn
as they start to channel
the ancient essence of
the storyteller

Little by little,
the others notice,
and they start to quiet down,
eager to begin

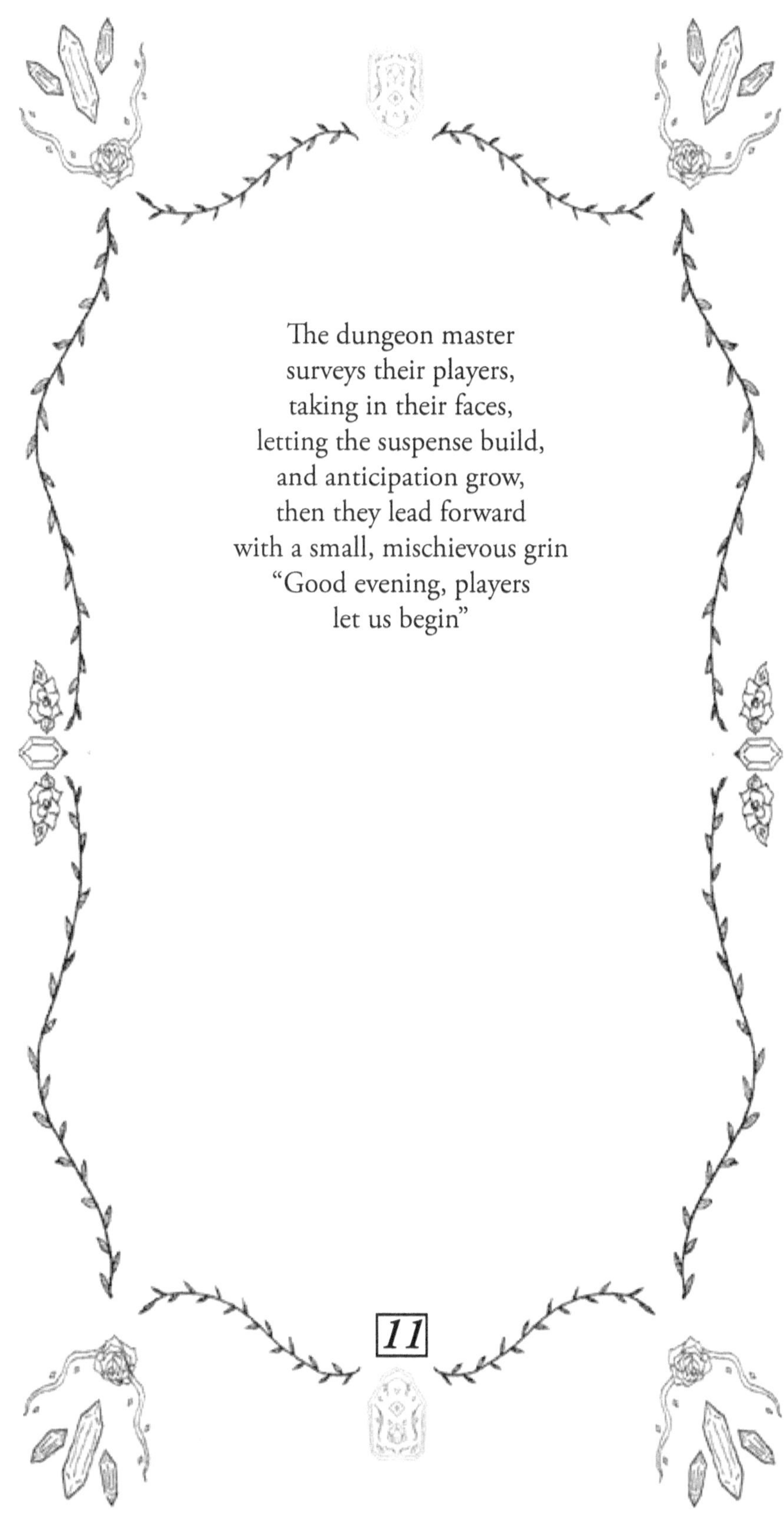

The dungeon master
surveys their players,
taking in their faces,
letting the suspense build,
and anticipation grow,
then they lead forward
with a small, mischievous grin
"Good evening, players
let us begin"

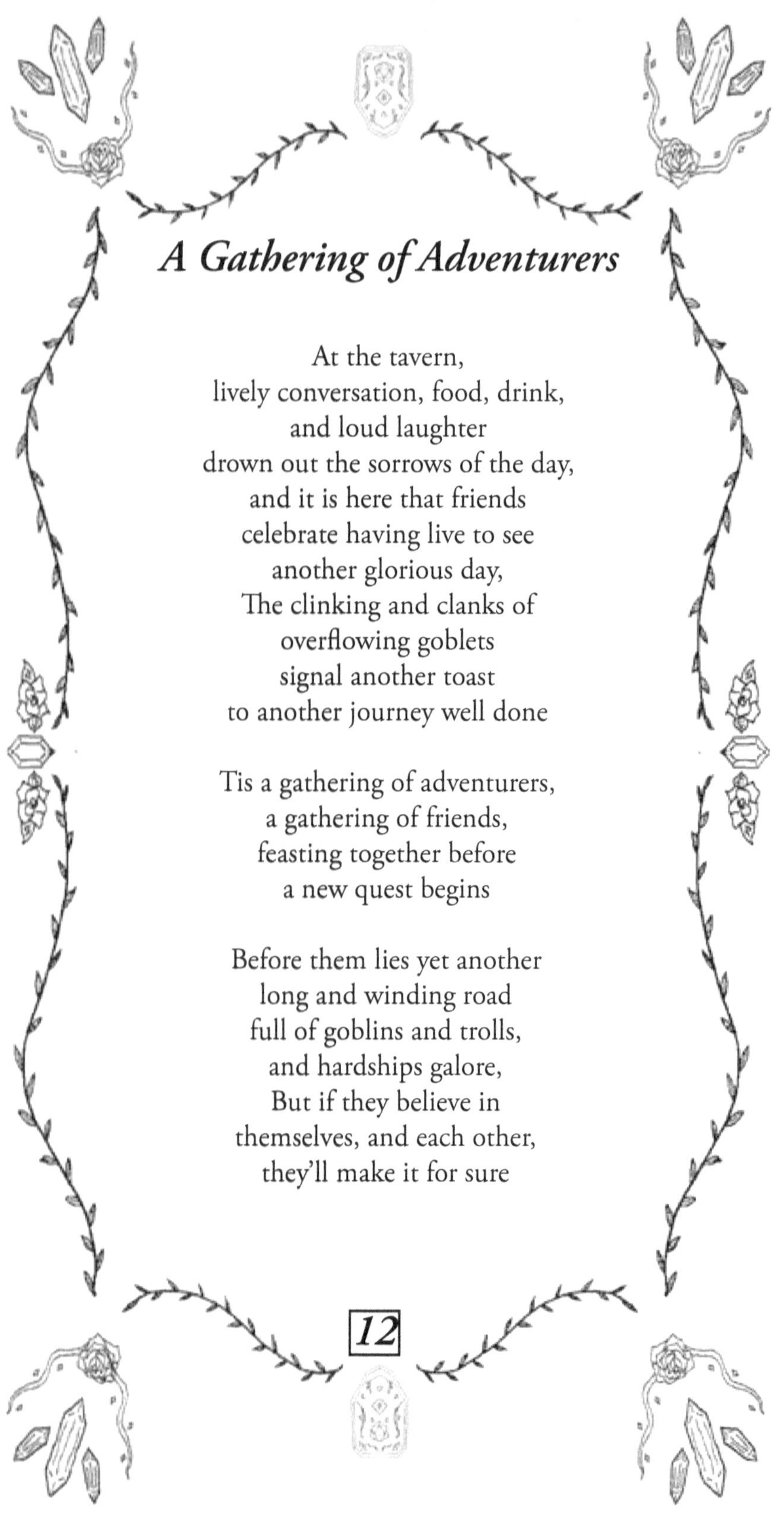

A Gathering of Adventurers

At the tavern,
lively conversation, food, drink,
and loud laughter
drown out the sorrows of the day,
and it is here that friends
celebrate having live to see
another glorious day,
The clinking and clanks of
overflowing goblets
signal another toast
to another journey well done

Tis a gathering of adventurers,
a gathering of friends,
feasting together before
a new quest begins

Before them lies yet another
long and winding road
full of goblins and trolls,
and hardships galore,
But if they believe in
themselves, and each other,
they'll make it for sure

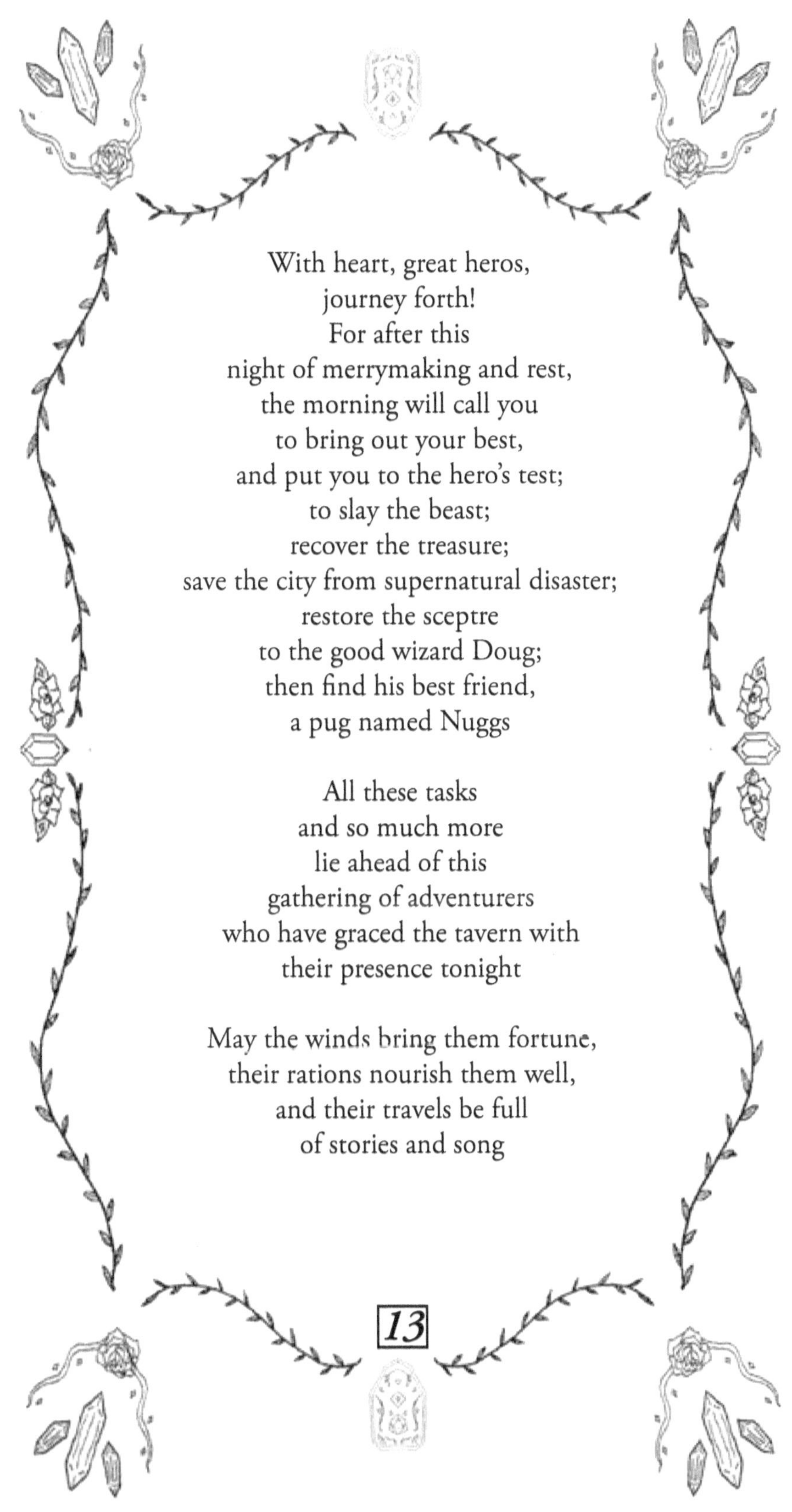

With heart, great heros,
journey forth!
For after this
night of merrymaking and rest,
the morning will call you
to bring out your best,
and put you to the hero's test;
to slay the beast;
recover the treasure;
save the city from supernatural disaster;
restore the sceptre
to the good wizard Doug;
then find his best friend,
a pug named Nuggs

All these tasks
and so much more
lie ahead of this
gathering of adventurers
who have graced the tavern with
their presence tonight

May the winds bring them fortune,
their rations nourish them well,
and their travels be full
of stories and song

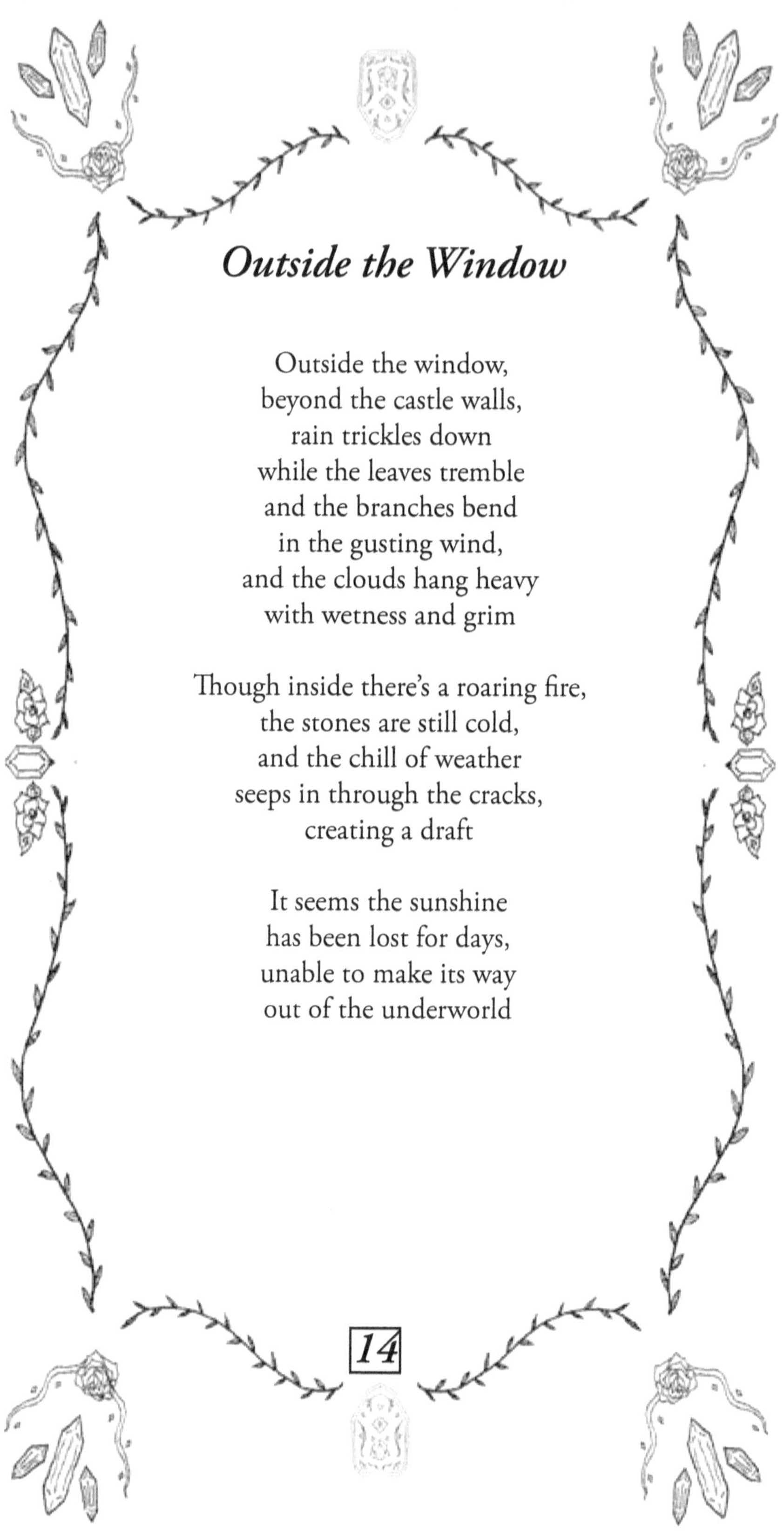

Outside the Window

Outside the window,
beyond the castle walls,
rain trickles down
while the leaves tremble
and the branches bend
in the gusting wind,
and the clouds hang heavy
with wetness and grim

Though inside there's a roaring fire,
the stones are still cold,
and the chill of weather
seeps in through the cracks,
creating a draft

It seems the sunshine
has been lost for days,
unable to make its way
out of the underworld

May be one day
there will be a rainbow,
Maybe one day,
the rain will go away
and the sun will find its way

Until then, I can only hold out hope
and keep the flames stoked

The Fairy's Last Wish

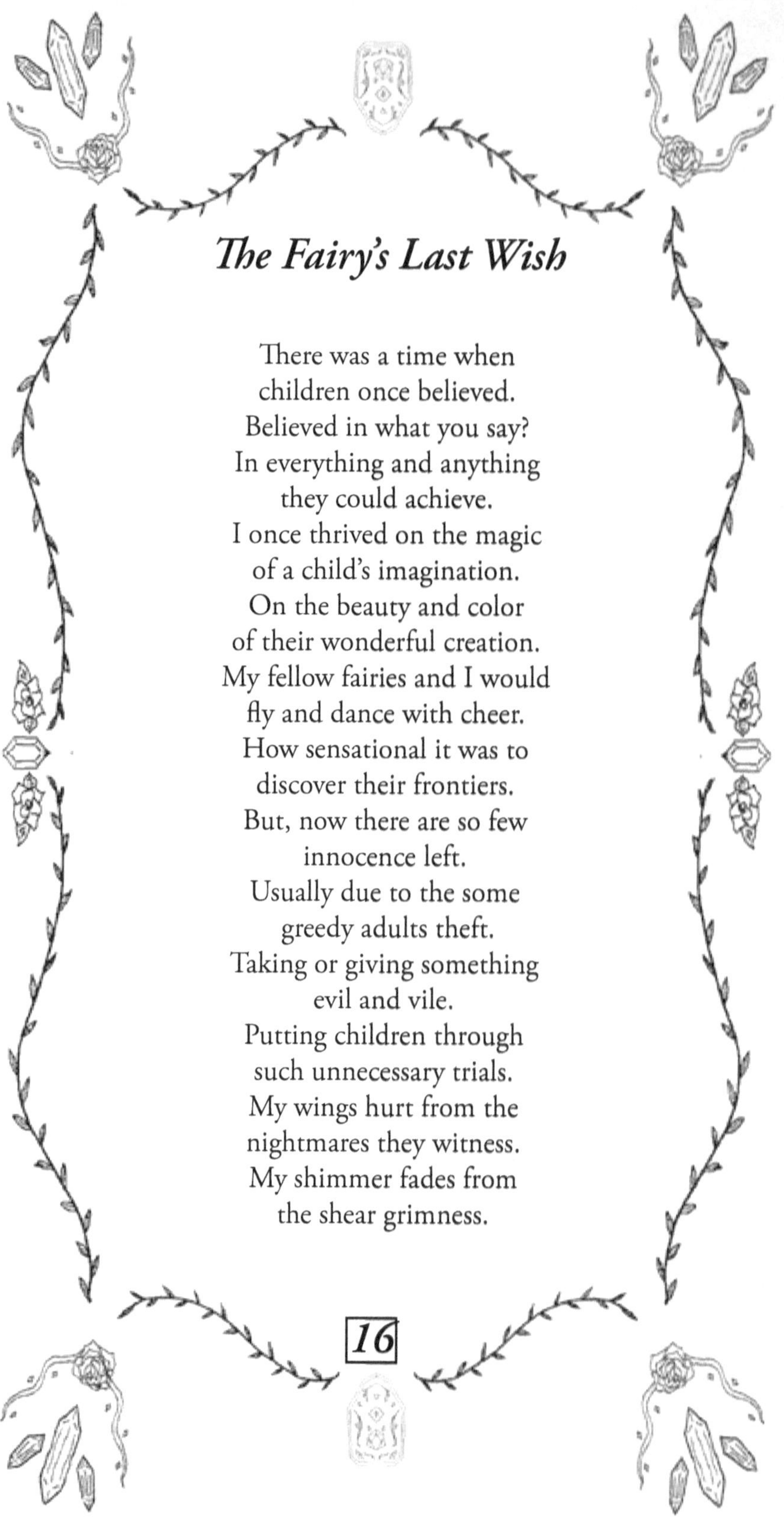

There was a time when
children once believed.
Believed in what you say?
In everything and anything
they could achieve.
I once thrived on the magic
of a child's imagination.
On the beauty and color
of their wonderful creation.
My fellow fairies and I would
fly and dance with cheer.
How sensational it was to
discover their frontiers.
But, now there are so few
innocence left.
Usually due to the some
greedy adults theft.
Taking or giving something
evil and vile.
Putting children through
such unnecessary trials.
My wings hurt from the
nightmares they witness.
My shimmer fades from
the shear grimness.

As I lay here now, in
my little nest.

I now realize that I'm
one of the last fairies left.
I am sending out my last
song tonight.
Hoping, praying that some
child might find the light.
"Keep on dreaming little ones,
Do not fear the cold and dark.
It is you who shapes the future
with your brilliant spark.
Sing, dance, and create your
extraordinary wonders.
Let it be heard like the
storm's rolling thunder."
I am getting cold now,
as pull on my leaf blanket.
I feel my soul begin
to enter transit.
Goodnight children from
now and forever.
One of these days, I hope
yours will better.
I bequeath my final
thoughts to you.
What sort of goals and
dreams will you renew?

By the Fireside

By the fireside,
Tales of all sorts are often told,
the legends of terror,
the sagas of heroes,
and accounts of romance,
the laments of loss,
the myths of the creatures
now hidden from our sights,
and the facts and the fictions of the lives
of the storytellers we gather around

And by the fireside
I stare into the flames,
and become entranced by a fiery world
where graceful figures dance,
whirling and twirling in the golden
courts of the sun king

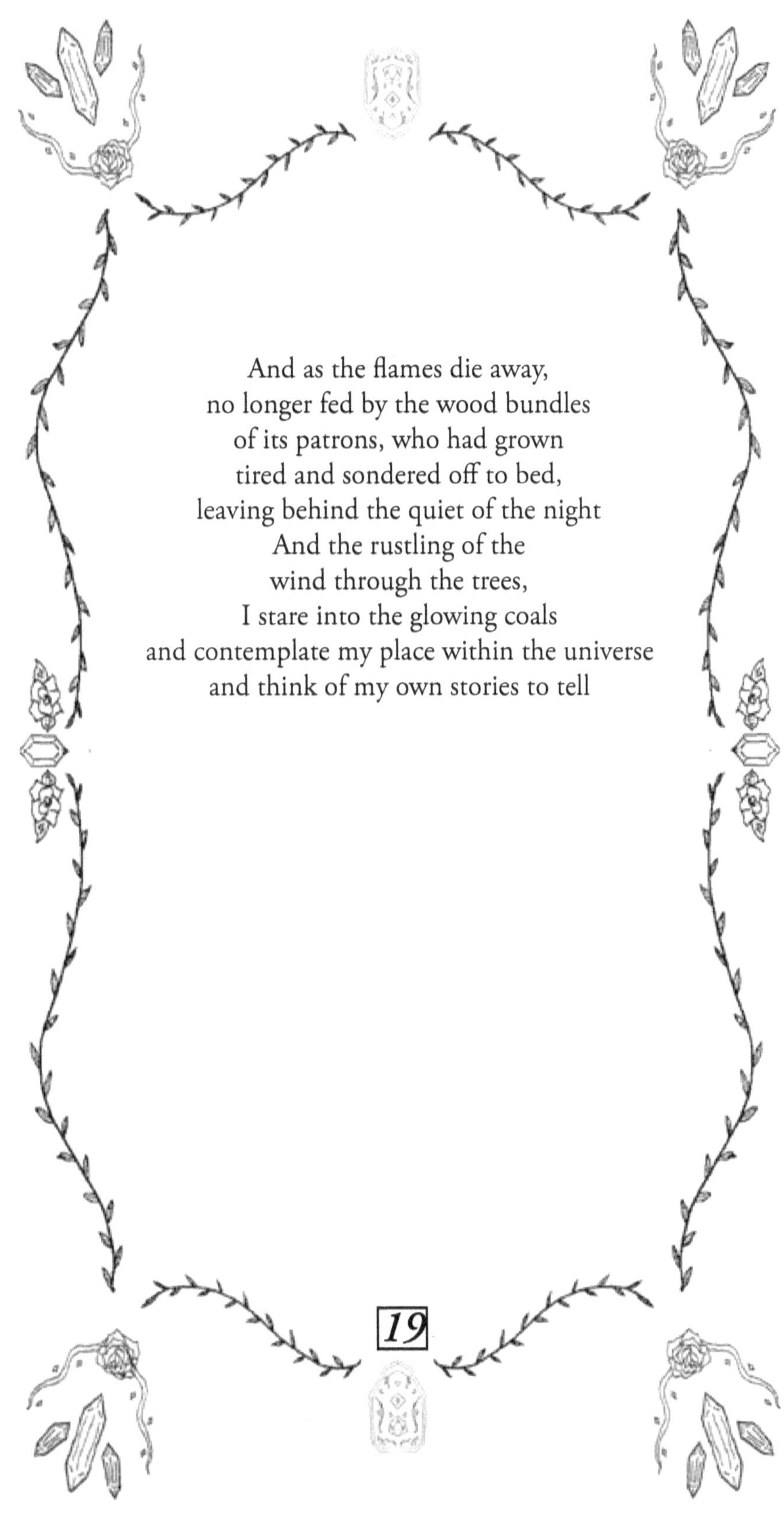

And as the flames die away,
no longer fed by the wood bundles
of its patrons, who had grown
tired and sondered off to bed,
leaving behind the quiet of the night
And the rustling of the
wind through the trees,
I stare into the glowing coals
and contemplate my place within the universe
and think of my own stories to tell

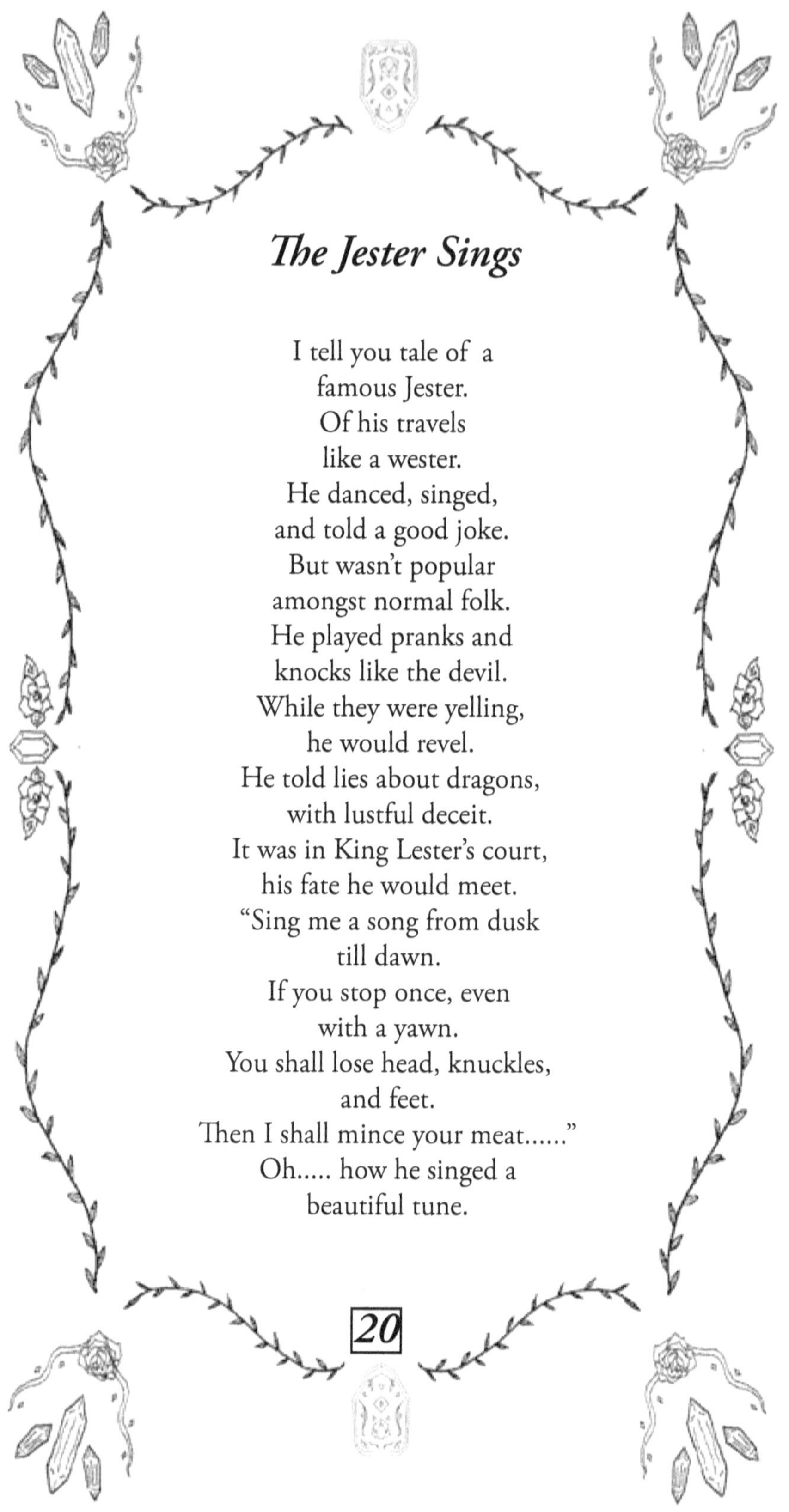

The Jester Sings

I tell you tale of a
famous Jester.
Of his travels
like a wester.
He danced, singed,
and told a good joke.
But wasn't popular
amongst normal folk.
He played pranks and
knocks like the devil.
While they were yelling,
he would revel.
He told lies about dragons,
with lustful deceit.
It was in King Lester's court,
his fate he would meet.
"Sing me a song from dusk
till dawn.
If you stop once, even
with a yawn.
You shall lose head, knuckles,
and feet.
Then I shall mince your meat......"
Oh..... how he singed a
beautiful tune.

All of the court ladies,
he did swoon.
But hours went by with
little to no rest.
The jester did know,
he had to do his best.
By morn, he was done.
but his was voice was gone.
He told no more lies, he
held his head in shame.
But he knew, he was the blame.
King Lester cried with so
much glee.
Knowing that the jester
had to bend the knee.
"Jester. Your lies and
tales of deceit.
Your forever silence
is your receipt."

Let Sleeping Dragons Lie

High in the mountains
where the memories live on.
The dragons still slumber beneath.
The ones we have lost.
The ones we had forgotten.
And the ones who foretold grief.
How they would dance in the
sky as they flew.
The smoke and flame from
the air they drew.
The kingdom's power was
laid to ash and soot.
As the beast's flames mocked
the structures they took.
After centries of dominance,
they were laid to rest.
In the caves they sleep, and wait.
But let their tales of glory live on, and
keep our imaginations awake.

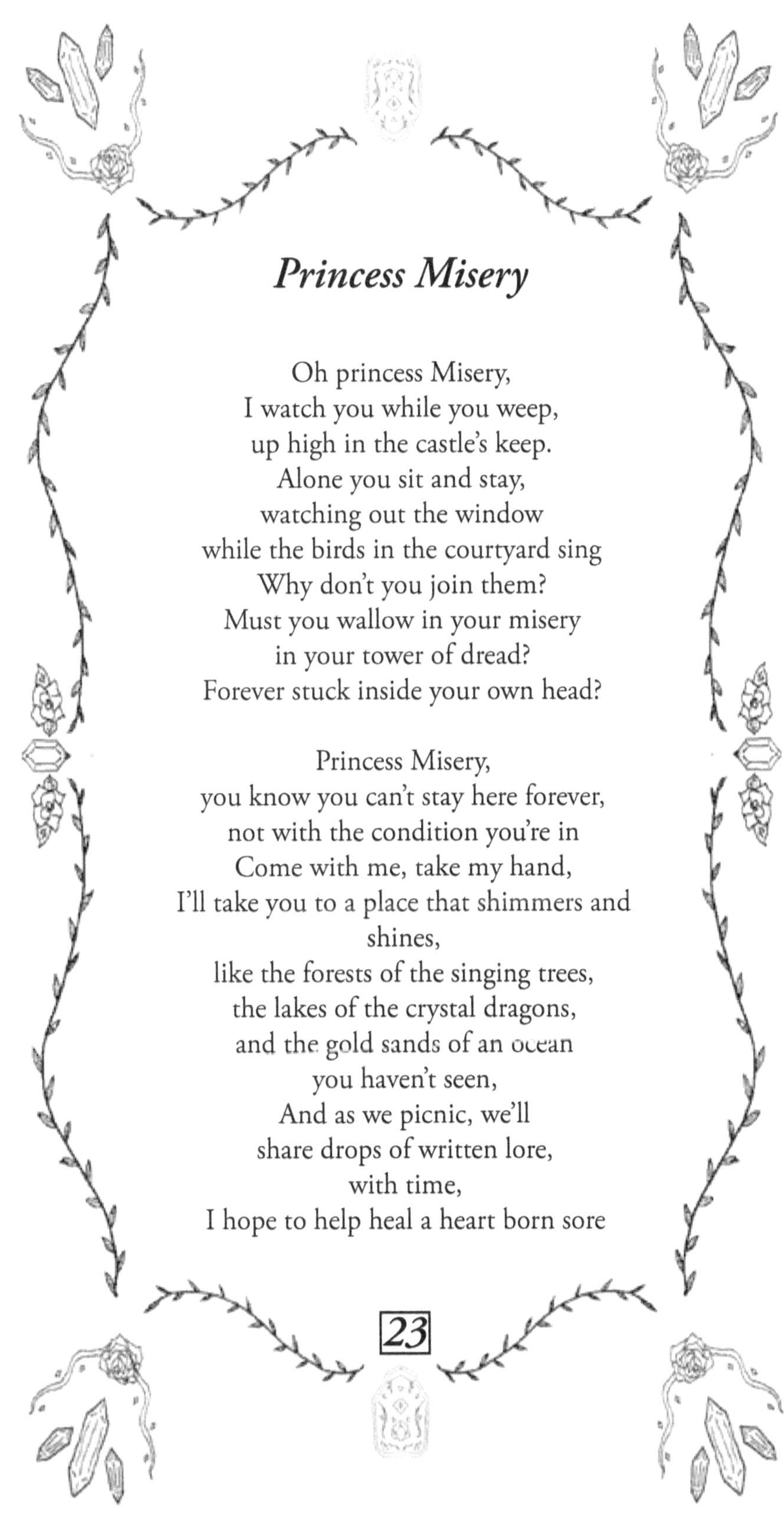

Princess Misery

Oh princess Misery,
I watch you while you weep,
up high in the castle's keep.
Alone you sit and stay,
watching out the window
while the birds in the courtyard sing
Why don't you join them?
Must you wallow in your misery
in your tower of dread?
Forever stuck inside your own head?

Princess Misery,
you know you can't stay here forever,
not with the condition you're in
Come with me, take my hand,
I'll take you to a place that shimmers and
shines,
like the forests of the singing trees,
the lakes of the crystal dragons,
and the gold sands of an ocean
you haven't seen,
And as we picnic, we'll
share drops of written lore,
with time,
I hope to help heal a heart born sore

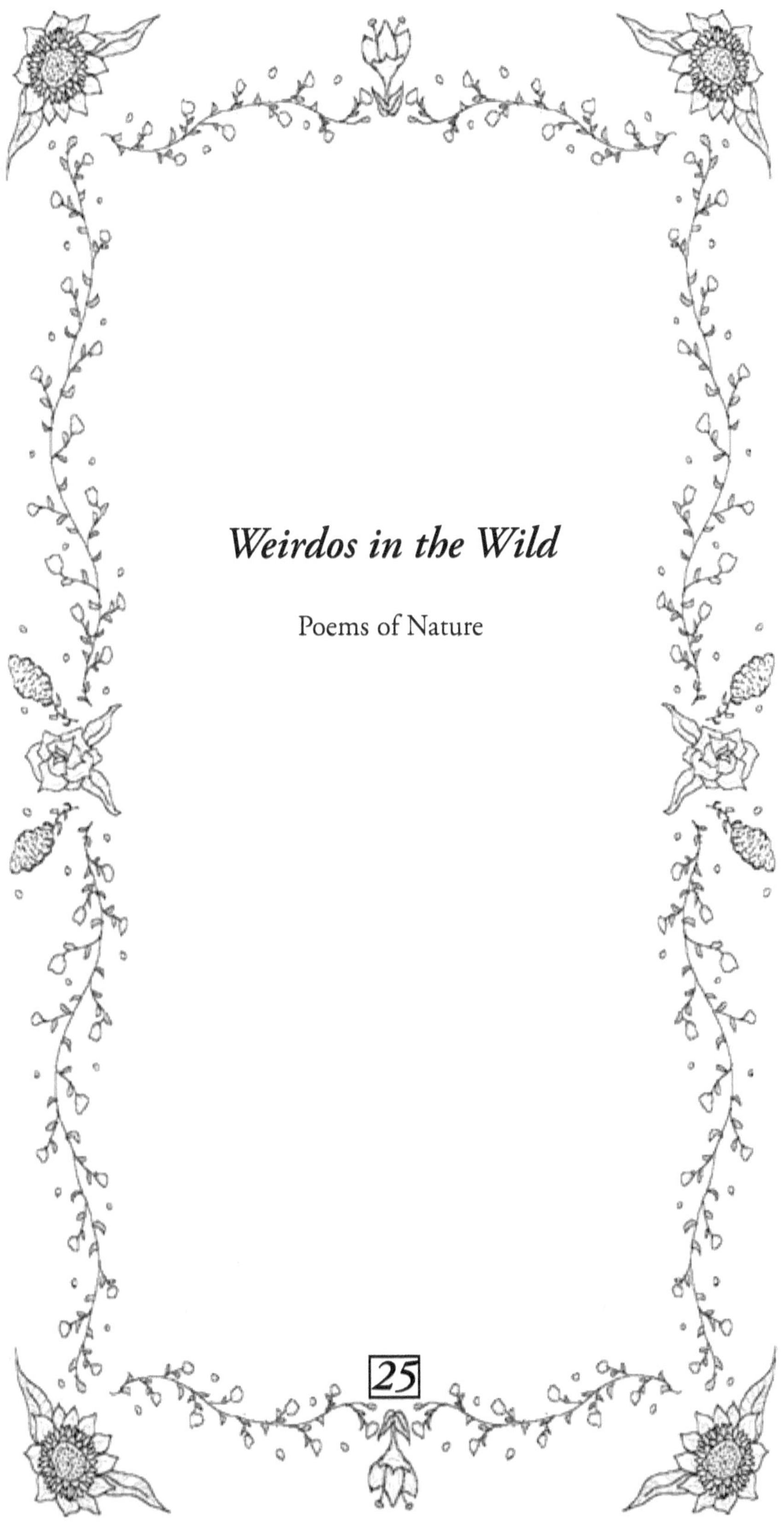

Weirdos in the Wild

Poems of Nature

25

In My Garden

In my garden,
things are overgrown.
The onions and rhubarb
went to seed,
the flowers went wild,
the cucumbers choked the peas,
the tomatoes ripened beautifully,
from green into a boisterous red,
but then they rotted away into a smelly mush
and fell into the dirt

It's only when things
got out of hand that
I thought that enough was enough
and tried to tame those stubborn plants
but my garden is vast and tangled
It's going to take some time…

And I think I'm going to
need assistance
weeding out the stink weeds
and the creeping charlies from the herbs

If I keep on it,
ask for help when I need it,
and choke out the guilt, not the growth
I could have a bountiful harvest
and happily share this little
garden I call my own

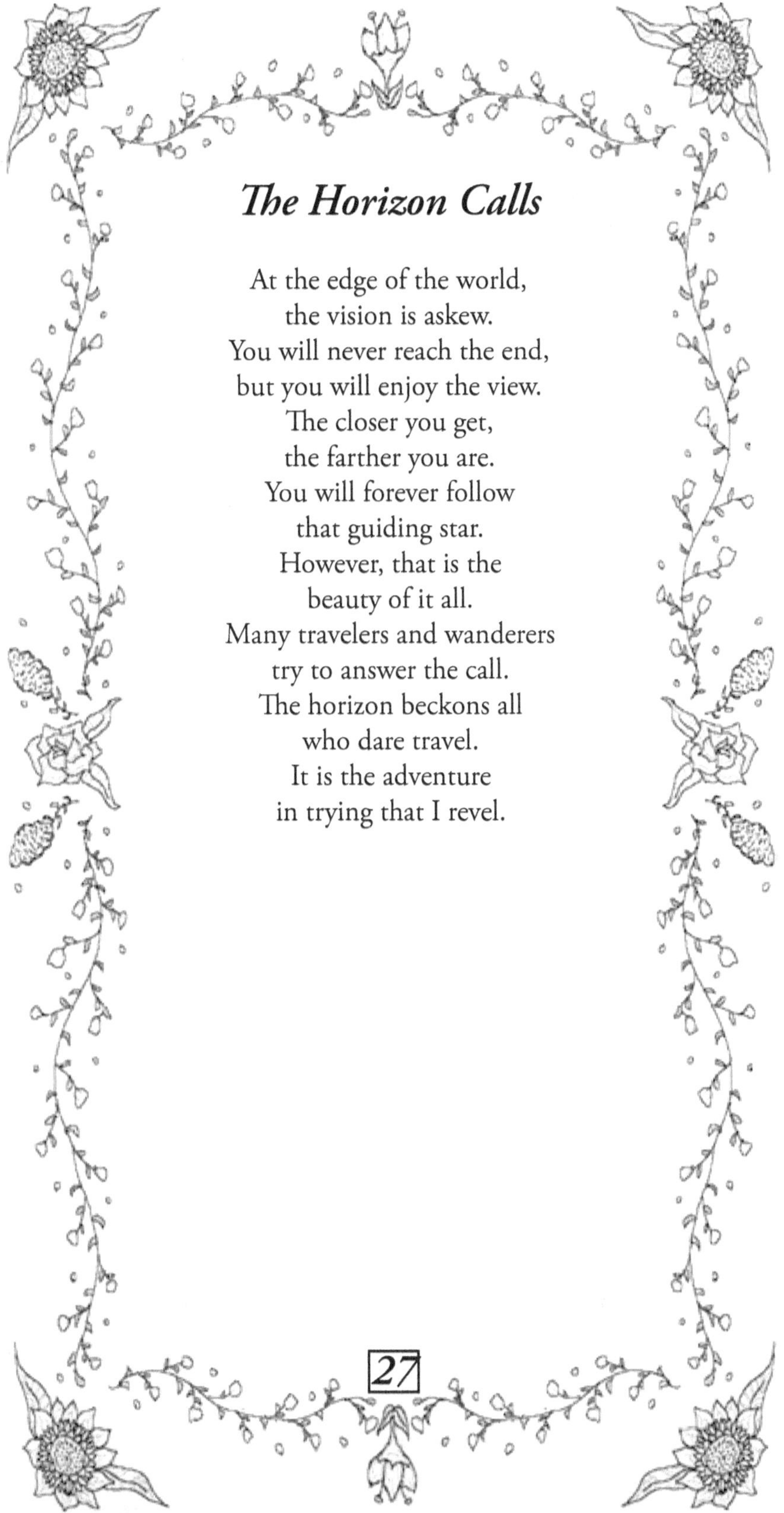

The Horizon Calls

At the edge of the world,
the vision is askew.
You will never reach the end,
but you will enjoy the view.
The closer you get,
the farther you are.
You will forever follow
that guiding star.
However, that is the
beauty of it all.
Many travelers and wanderers
try to answer the call.
The horizon beckons all
who dare travel.
It is the adventure
in trying that I revel.

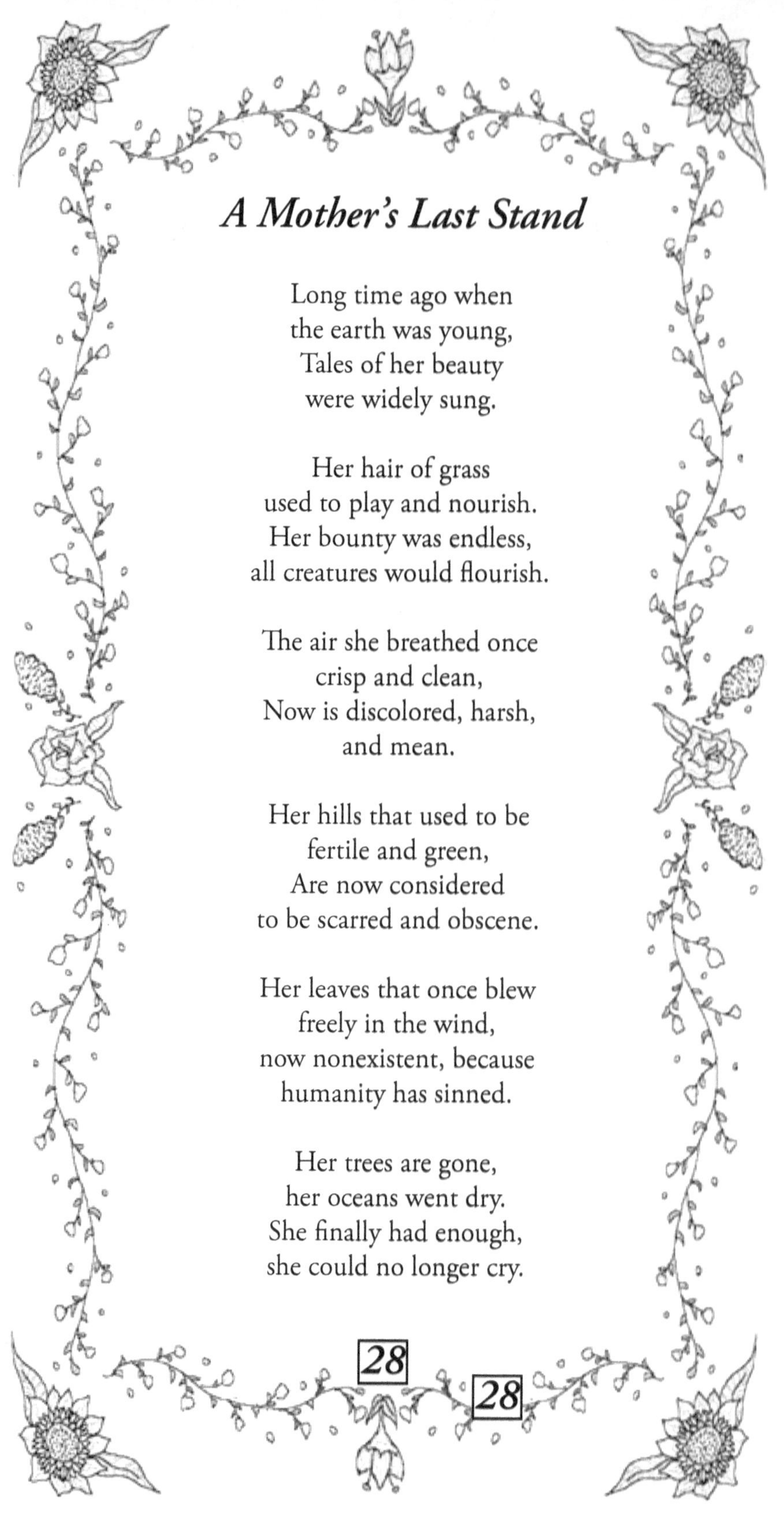

A Mother's Last Stand

Long time ago when
the earth was young,
Tales of her beauty
were widely sung.

Her hair of grass
used to play and nourish.
Her bounty was endless,
all creatures would flourish.

The air she breathed once
crisp and clean,
Now is discolored, harsh,
and mean.

Her hills that used to be
fertile and green,
Are now considered
to be scarred and obscene.

Her leaves that once blew
freely in the wind,
now nonexistent, because
humanity has sinned.

Her trees are gone,
her oceans went dry.
She finally had enough,
she could no longer cry.

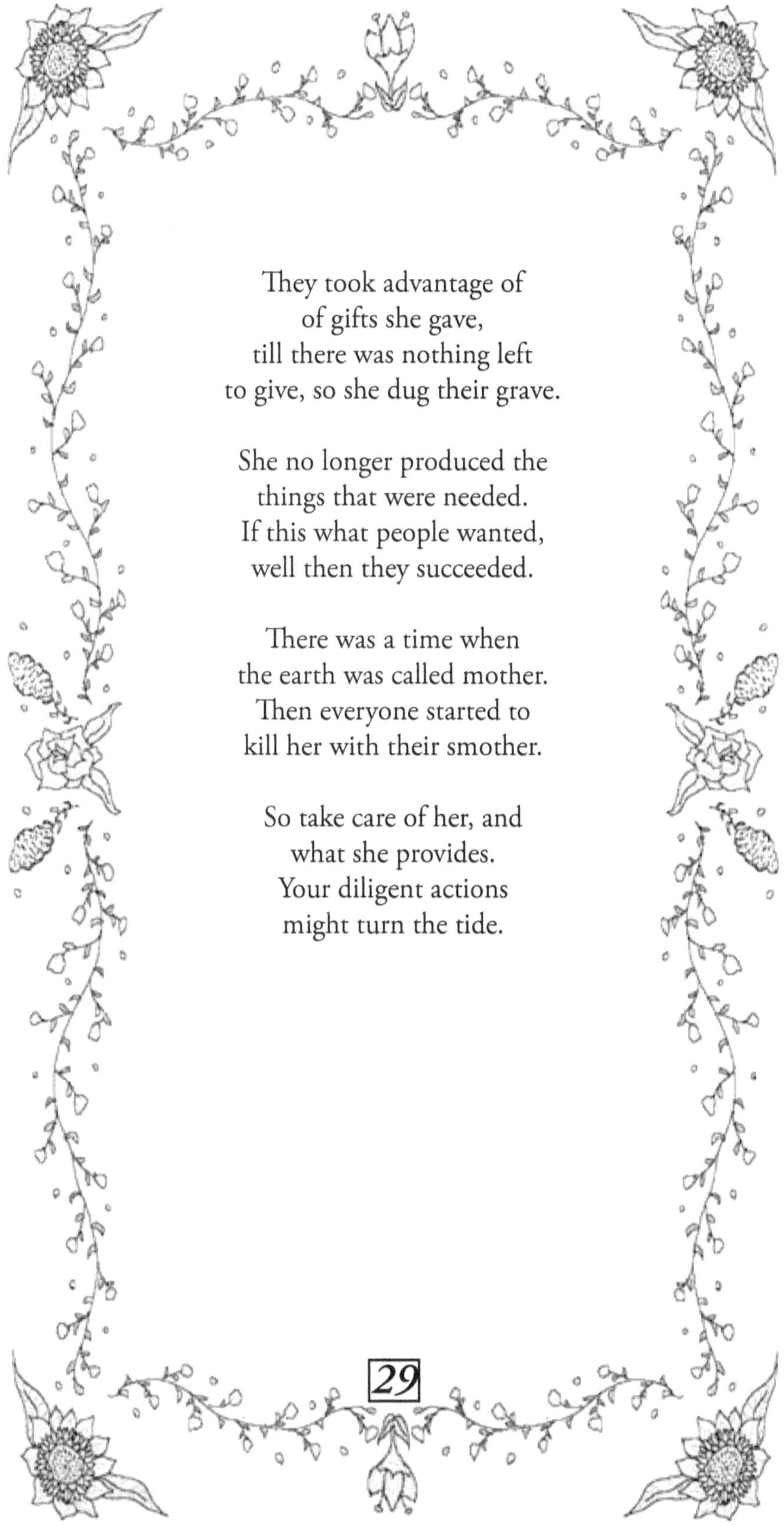

They took advantage of
of gifts she gave,
till there was nothing left
to give, so she dug their grave.

She no longer produced the
things that were needed.
If this what people wanted,
well then they succeeded.

There was a time when
the earth was called mother.
Then everyone started to
kill her with their smother.

So take care of her, and
what she provides.
Your diligent actions
might turn the tide.

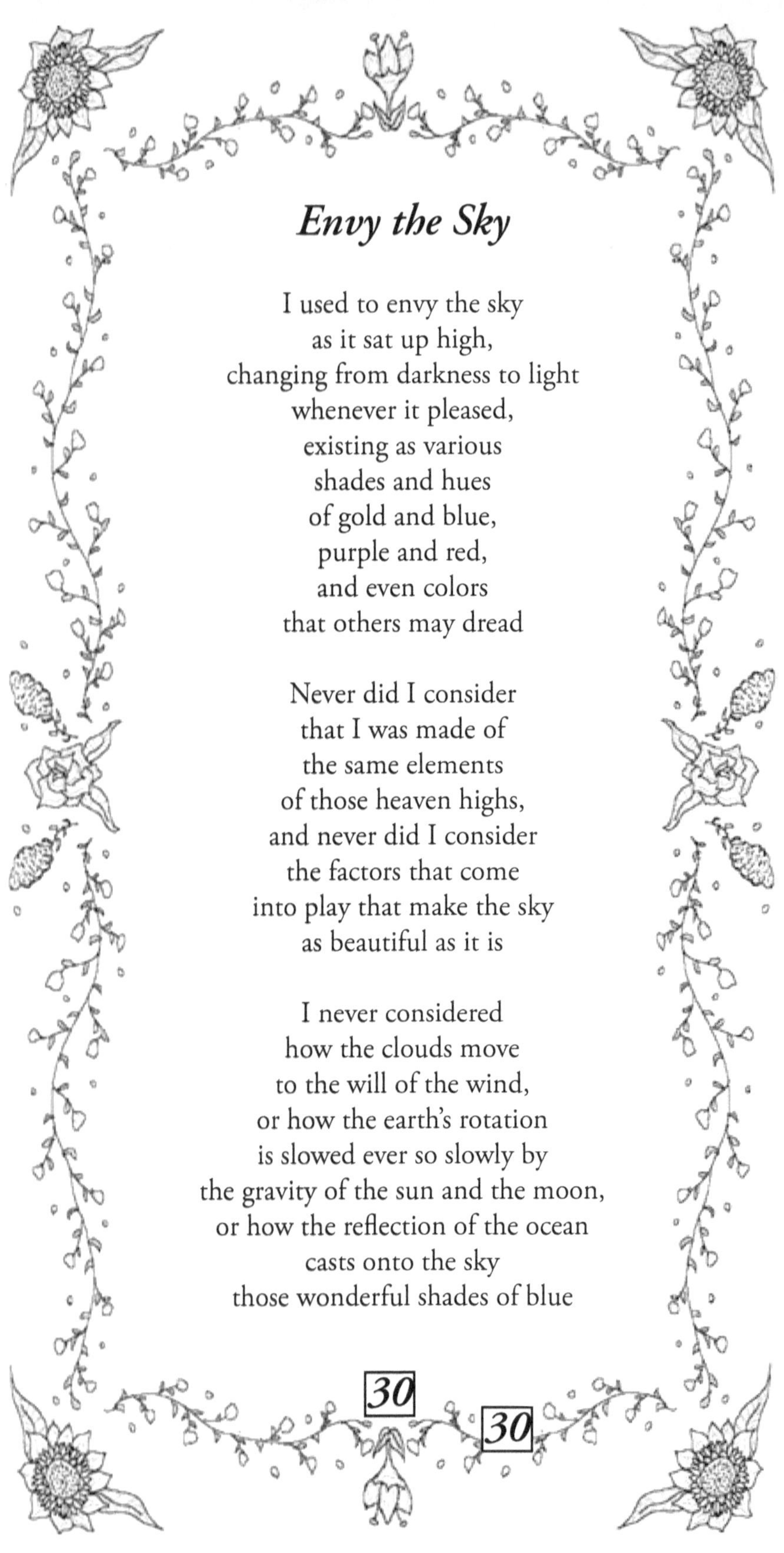

Envy the Sky

I used to envy the sky
as it sat up high,
changing from darkness to light
whenever it pleased,
existing as various
shades and hues
of gold and blue,
purple and red,
and even colors
that others may dread

Never did I consider
that I was made of
the same elements
of those heaven highs,
and never did I consider
the factors that come
into play that make the sky
as beautiful as it is

I never considered
how the clouds move
to the will of the wind,
or how the earth's rotation
is slowed ever so slowly by
the gravity of the sun and the moon,
or how the reflection of the ocean
casts onto the sky
those wonderful shades of blue

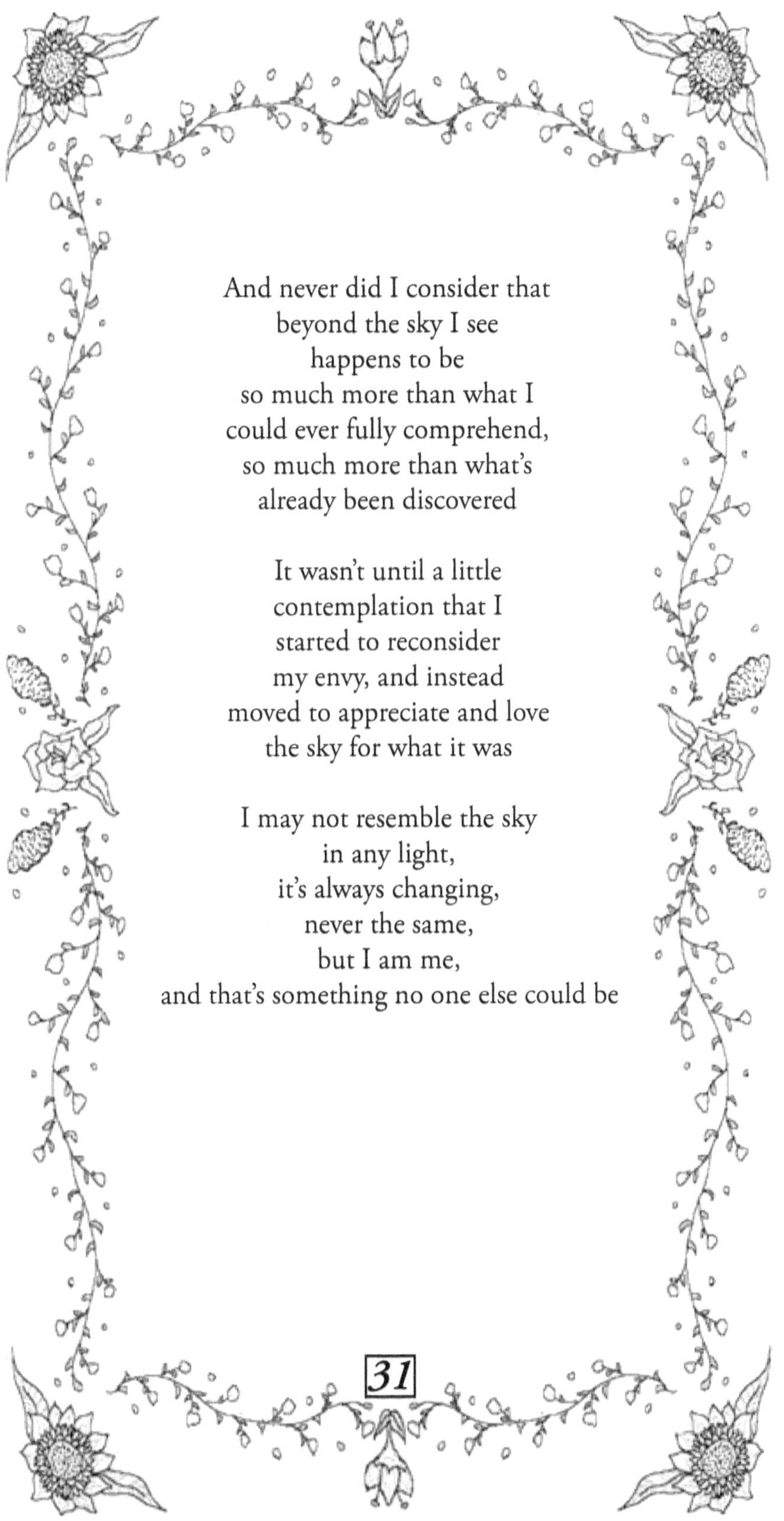

And never did I consider that
beyond the sky I see
happens to be
so much more than what I
could ever fully comprehend,
so much more than what's
already been discovered

It wasn't until a little
contemplation that I
started to reconsider
my envy, and instead
moved to appreciate and love
the sky for what it was

I may not resemble the sky
in any light,
it's always changing,
never the same,
but I am me,
and that's something no one else could be

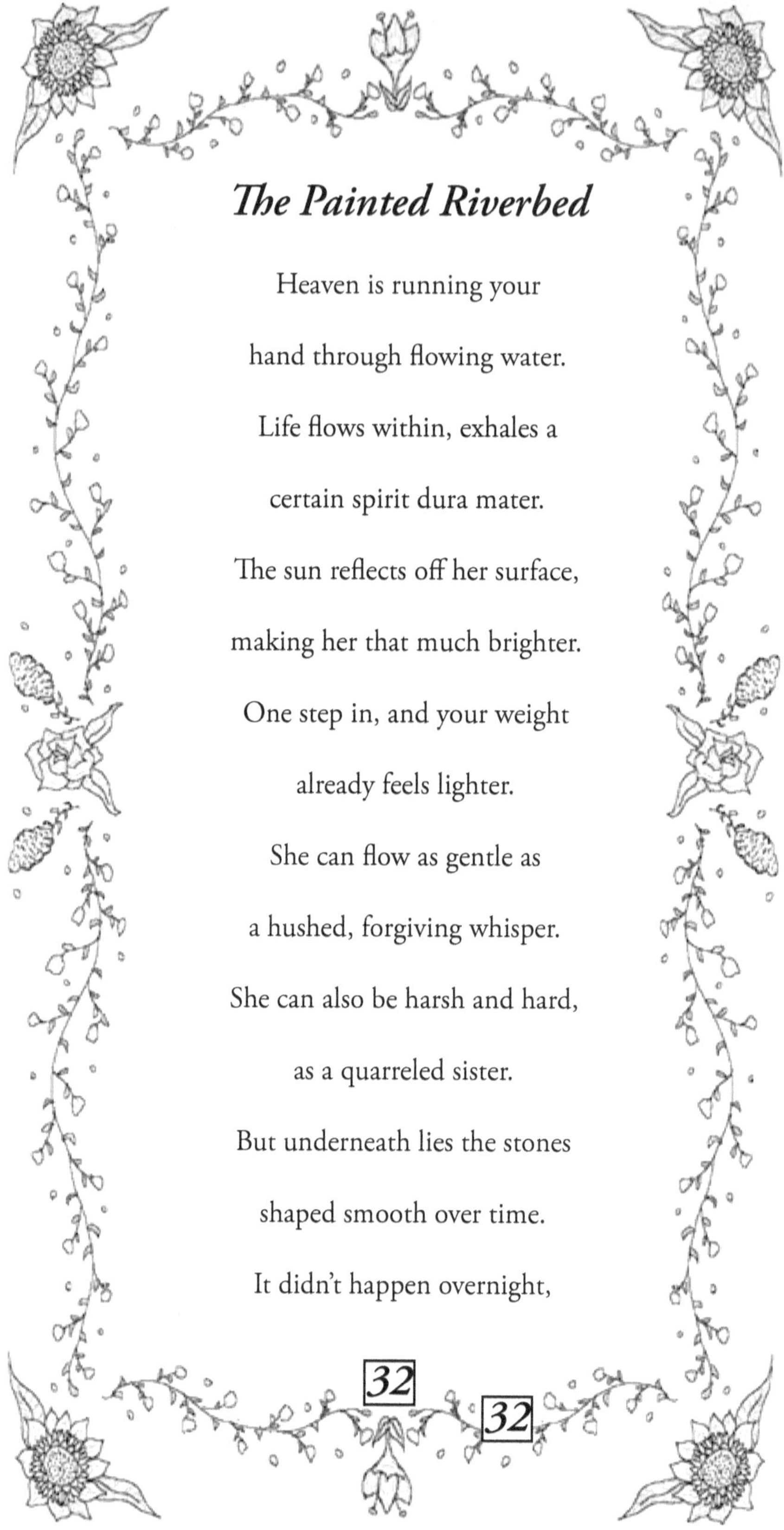

The Painted Riverbed

Heaven is running your

hand through flowing water.

Life flows within, exhales a

certain spirit dura mater.

The sun reflects off her surface,

making her that much brighter.

One step in, and your weight

already feels lighter.

She can flow as gentle as

a hushed, forgiving whisper.

She can also be harsh and hard,

as a quarreled sister.

But underneath lies the stones

shaped smooth over time.

It didn't happen overnight,

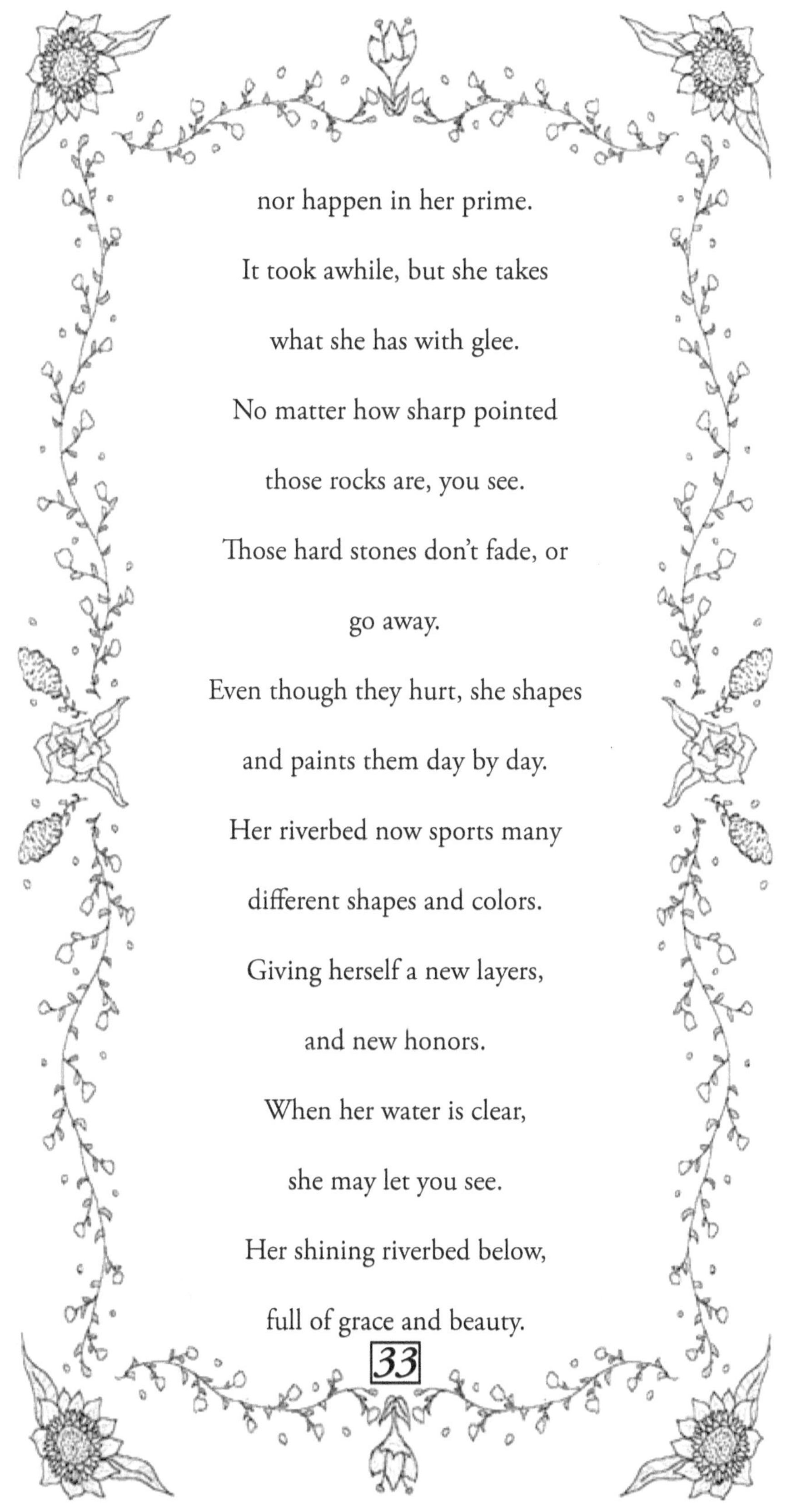

nor happen in her prime.

It took awhile, but she takes

what she has with glee.

No matter how sharp pointed

those rocks are, you see.

Those hard stones don't fade, or

go away.

Even though they hurt, she shapes

and paints them day by day.

Her riverbed now sports many

different shapes and colors.

Giving herself a new layers,

and new honors.

When her water is clear,

she may let you see.

Her shining riverbed below,

full of grace and beauty.

33

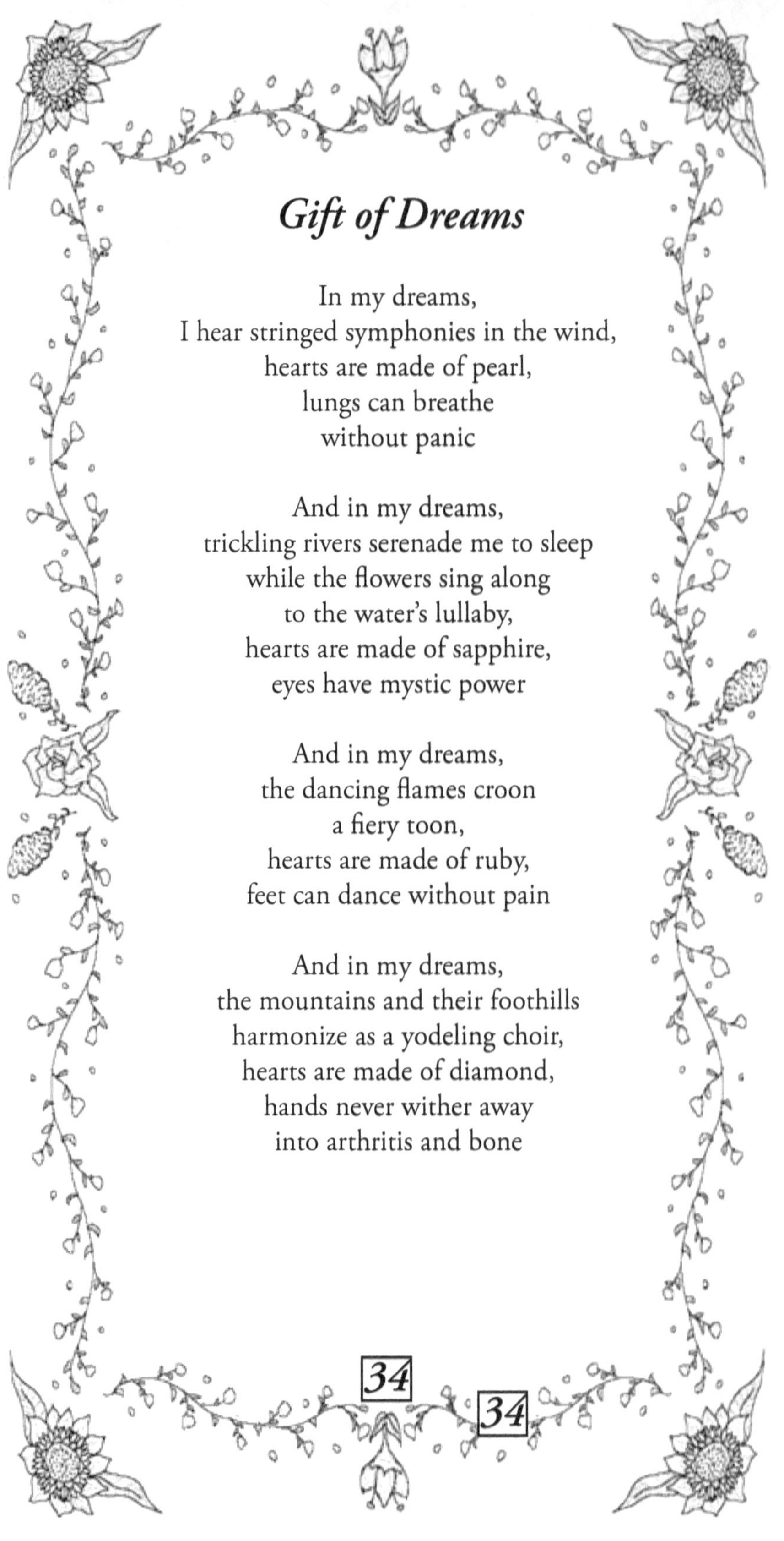

Gift of Dreams

In my dreams,
I hear stringed symphonies in the wind,
hearts are made of pearl,
lungs can breathe
without panic

And in my dreams,
trickling rivers serenade me to sleep
while the flowers sing along
to the water's lullaby,
hearts are made of sapphire,
eyes have mystic power

And in my dreams,
the dancing flames croon
a fiery toon,
hearts are made of ruby,
feet can dance without pain

And in my dreams,
the mountains and their foothills
harmonize as a yodeling choir,
hearts are made of diamond,
hands never wither away
into arthritis and bone

And in my dreams,
we all come together
for the sake of a song,
hearts are made of gold and silver,
veins are made of rainbows,
and love can be found all around

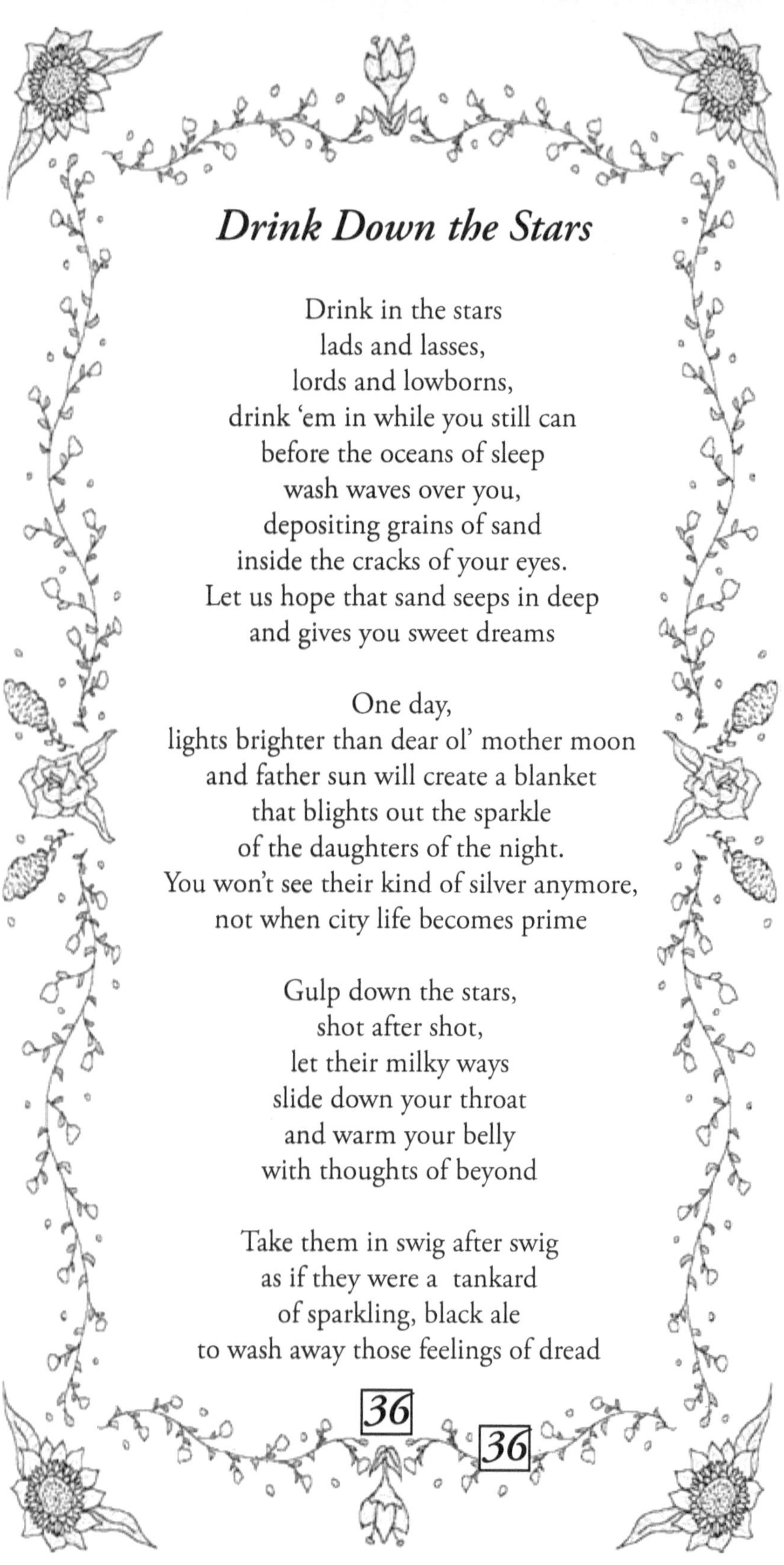

Drink Down the Stars

Drink in the stars
lads and lasses,
lords and lowborns,
drink 'em in while you still can
before the oceans of sleep
wash waves over you,
depositing grains of sand
inside the cracks of your eyes.
Let us hope that sand seeps in deep
and gives you sweet dreams

One day,
lights brighter than dear ol' mother moon
and father sun will create a blanket
that blights out the sparkle
of the daughters of the night.
You won't see their kind of silver anymore,
not when city life becomes prime

Gulp down the stars,
shot after shot,
let their milky ways
slide down your throat
and warm your belly
with thoughts of beyond

Take them in swig after swig
as if they were a tankard
of sparkling, black ale
to wash away those feelings of dread

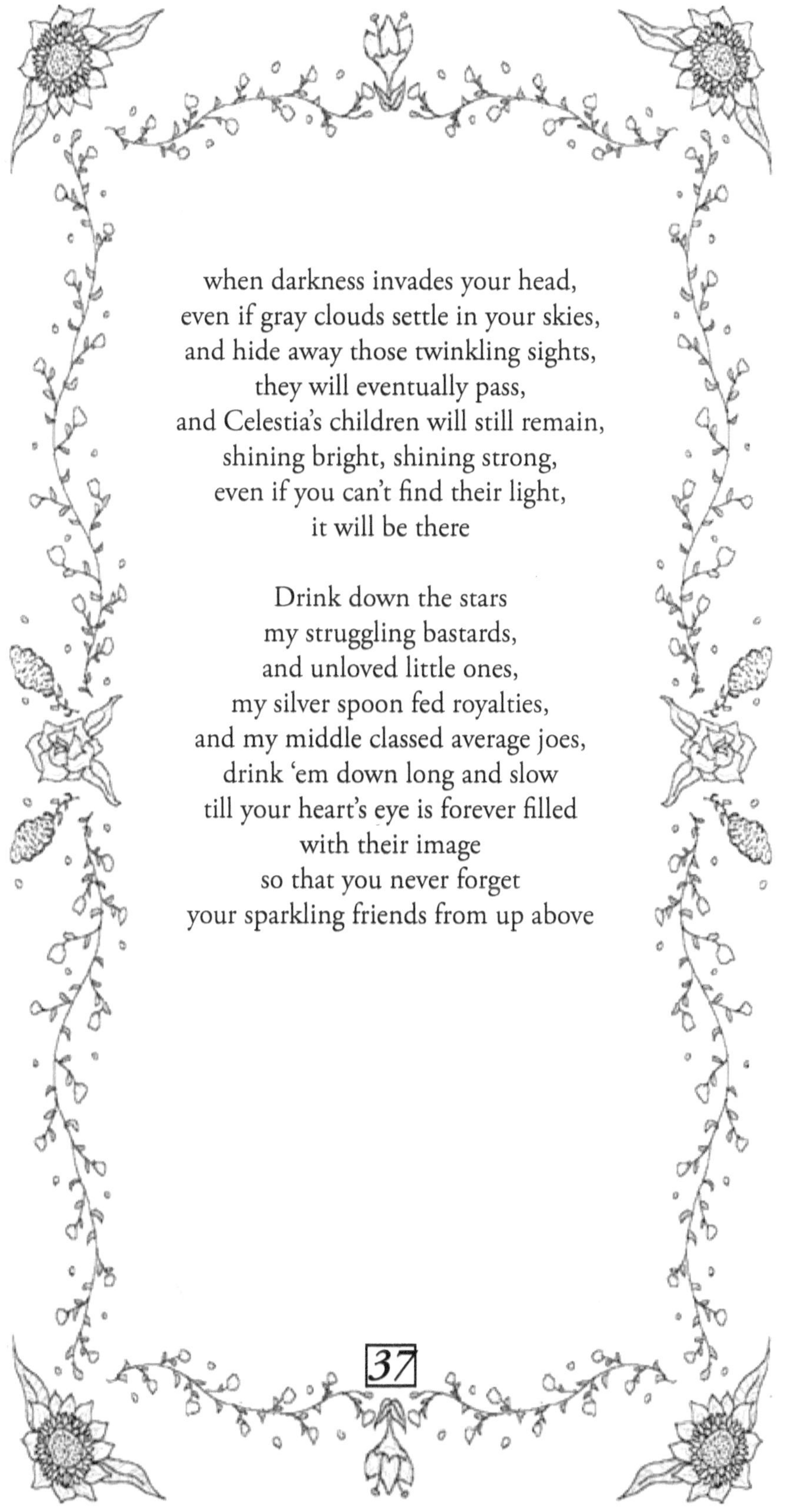

when darkness invades your head,
even if gray clouds settle in your skies,
and hide away those twinkling sights,
they will eventually pass,
and Celestia's children will still remain,
shining bright, shining strong,
even if you can't find their light,
it will be there

Drink down the stars
my struggling bastards,
and unloved little ones,
my silver spoon fed royalties,
and my middle classed average joes,
drink 'em down long and slow
till your heart's eye is forever filled
with their image
so that you never forget
your sparkling friends from up above

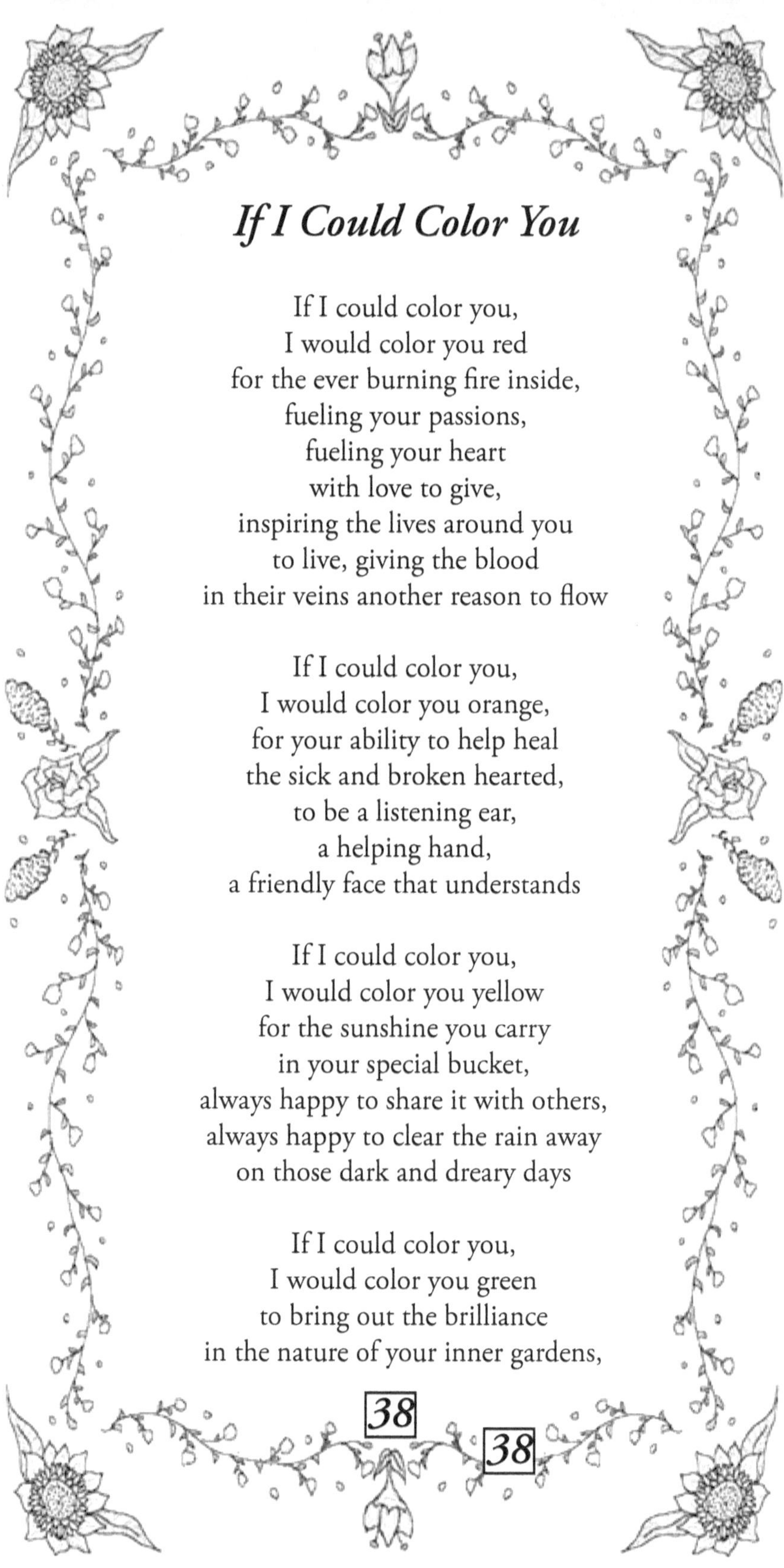

If I Could Color You

If I could color you,
I would color you red
for the ever burning fire inside,
fueling your passions,
fueling your heart
with love to give,
inspiring the lives around you
to live, giving the blood
in their veins another reason to flow

If I could color you,
I would color you orange,
for your ability to help heal
the sick and broken hearted,
to be a listening ear,
a helping hand,
a friendly face that understands

If I could color you,
I would color you yellow
for the sunshine you carry
in your special bucket,
always happy to share it with others,
always happy to clear the rain away
on those dark and dreary days

If I could color you,
I would color you green
to bring out the brilliance
in the nature of your inner gardens,

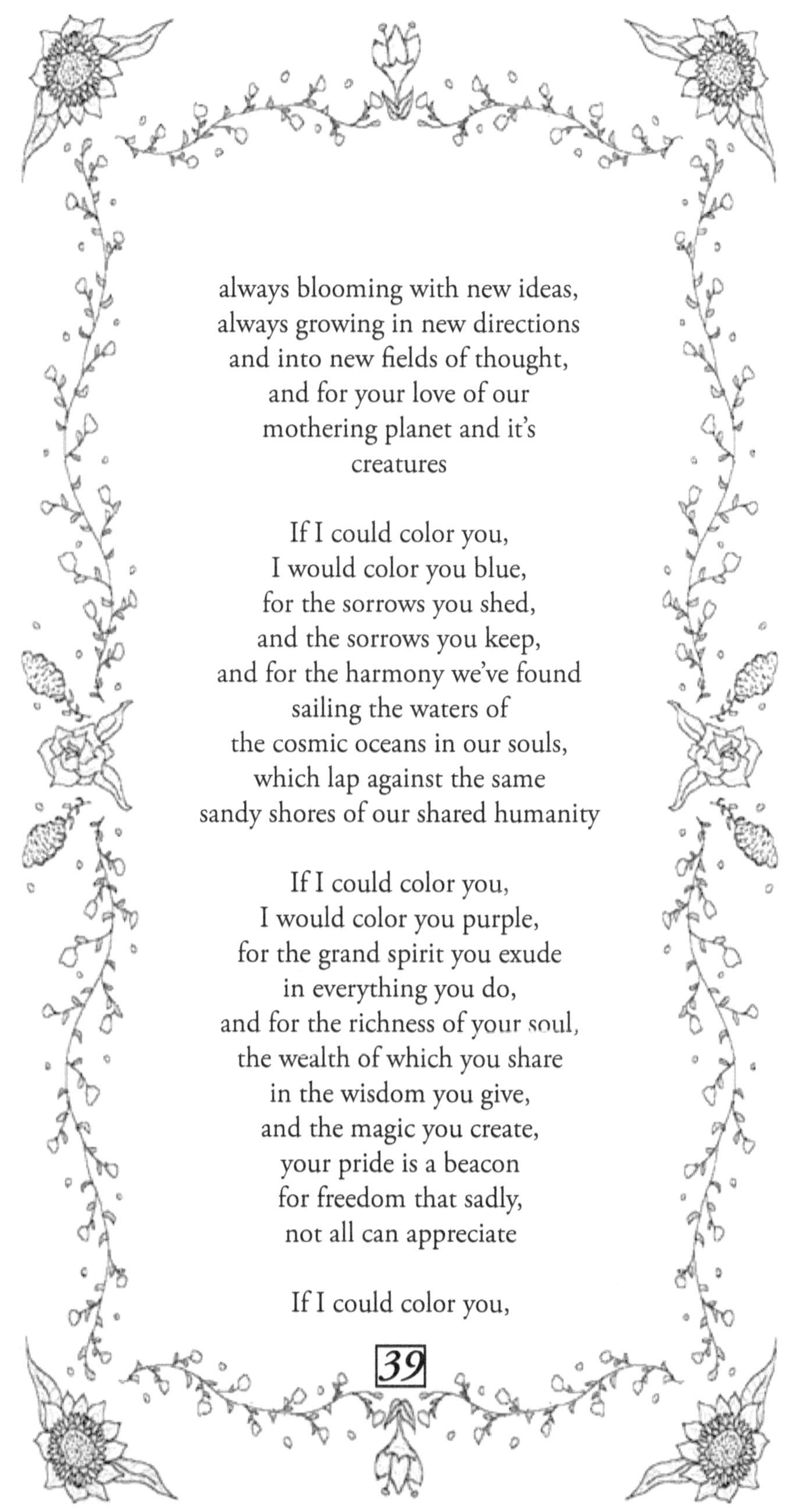

always blooming with new ideas,
always growing in new directions
and into new fields of thought,
and for your love of our
mothering planet and it's
creatures

If I could color you,
I would color you blue,
for the sorrows you shed,
and the sorrows you keep,
and for the harmony we've found
sailing the waters of
the cosmic oceans in our souls,
which lap against the same
sandy shores of our shared humanity

If I could color you,
I would color you purple,
for the grand spirit you exude
in everything you do,
and for the richness of your soul,
the wealth of which you share
in the wisdom you give,
and the magic you create,
your pride is a beacon
for freedom that sadly,
not all can appreciate

If I could color you,

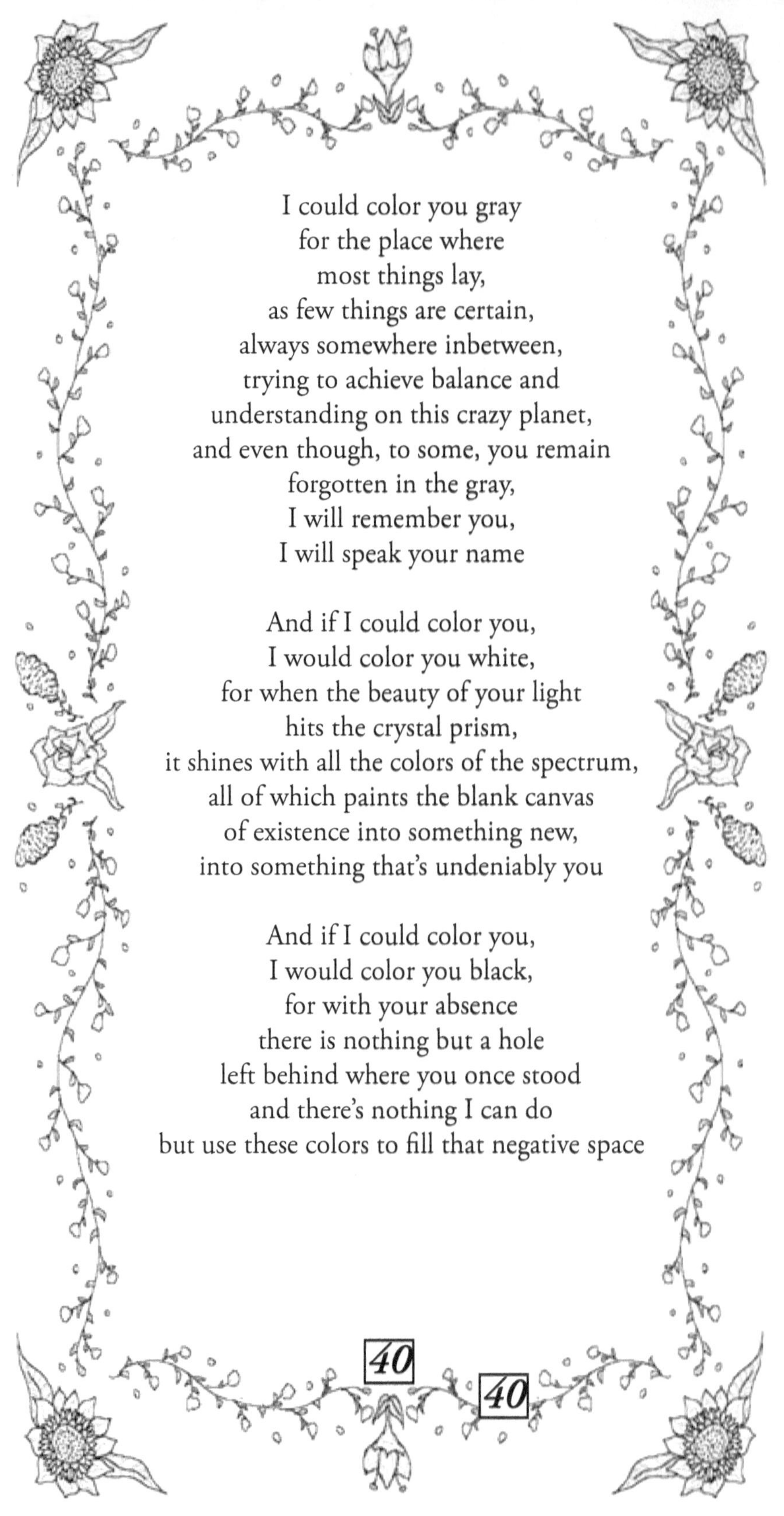

I could color you gray
for the place where
most things lay,
as few things are certain,
always somewhere inbetween,
trying to achieve balance and
understanding on this crazy planet,
and even though, to some, you remain
forgotten in the gray,
I will remember you,
I will speak your name

And if I could color you,
I would color you white,
for when the beauty of your light
hits the crystal prism,
it shines with all the colors of the spectrum,
all of which paints the blank canvas
of existence into something new,
into something that's undeniably you

And if I could color you,
I would color you black,
for with your absence
there is nothing but a hole
left behind where you once stood
and there's nothing I can do
but use these colors to fill that negative space

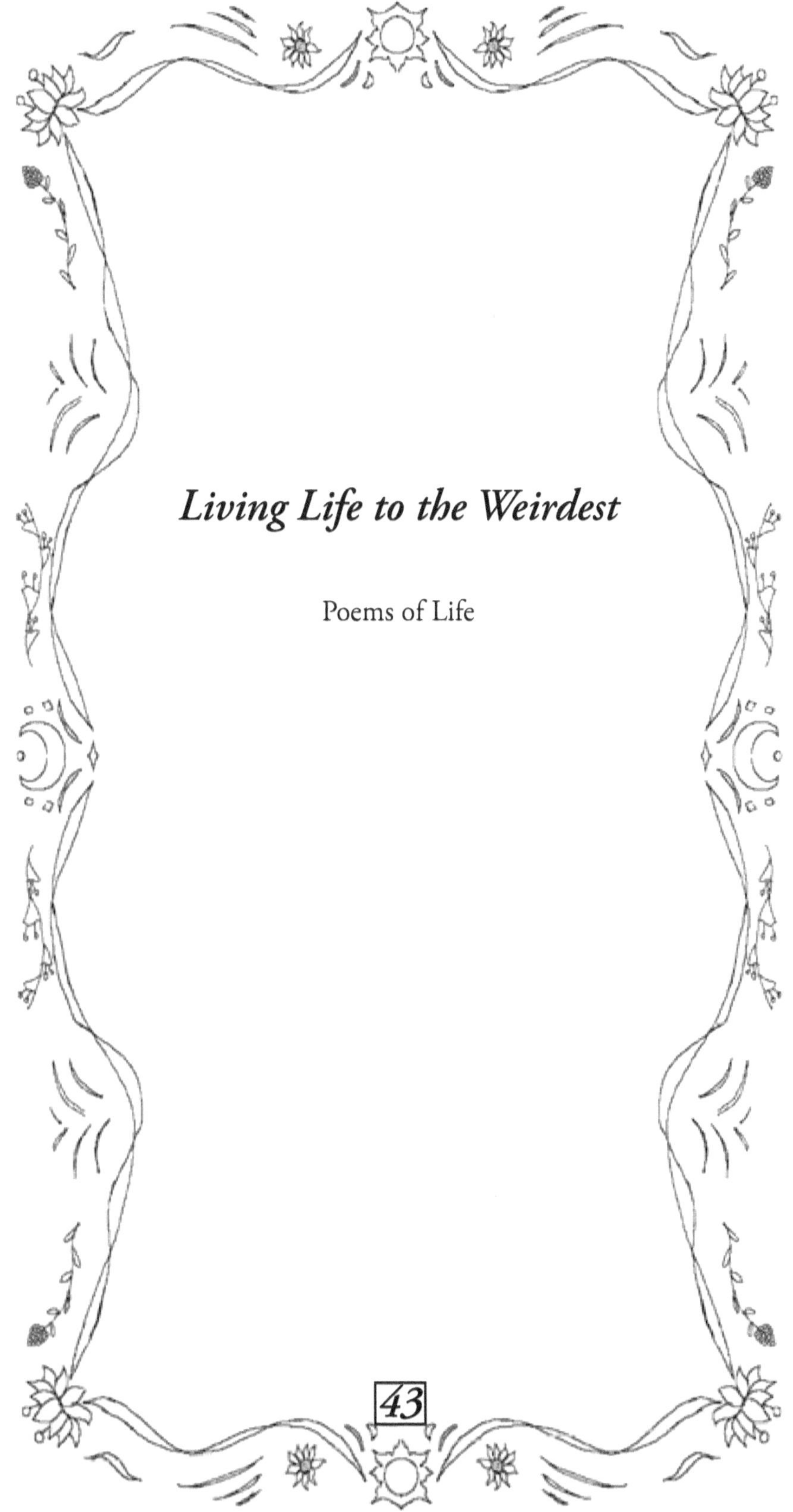

Living Life to the Weirdest

Poems of Life

43

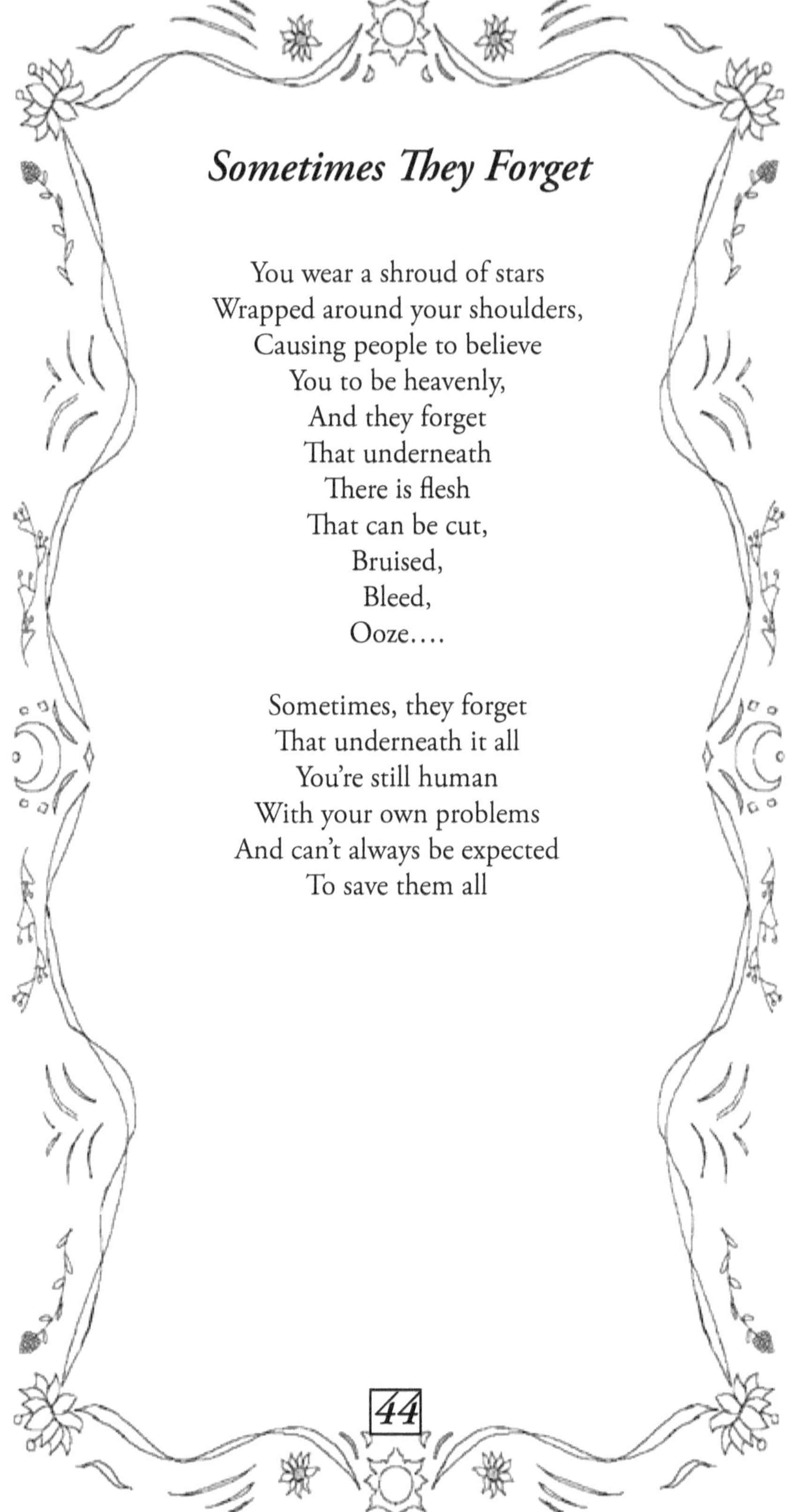

Sometimes They Forget

You wear a shroud of stars
Wrapped around your shoulders,
Causing people to believe
You to be heavenly,
And they forget
That underneath
There is flesh
That can be cut,
Bruised,
Bleed,
Ooze….

Sometimes, they forget
That underneath it all
You're still human
With your own problems
And can't always be expected
To save them all

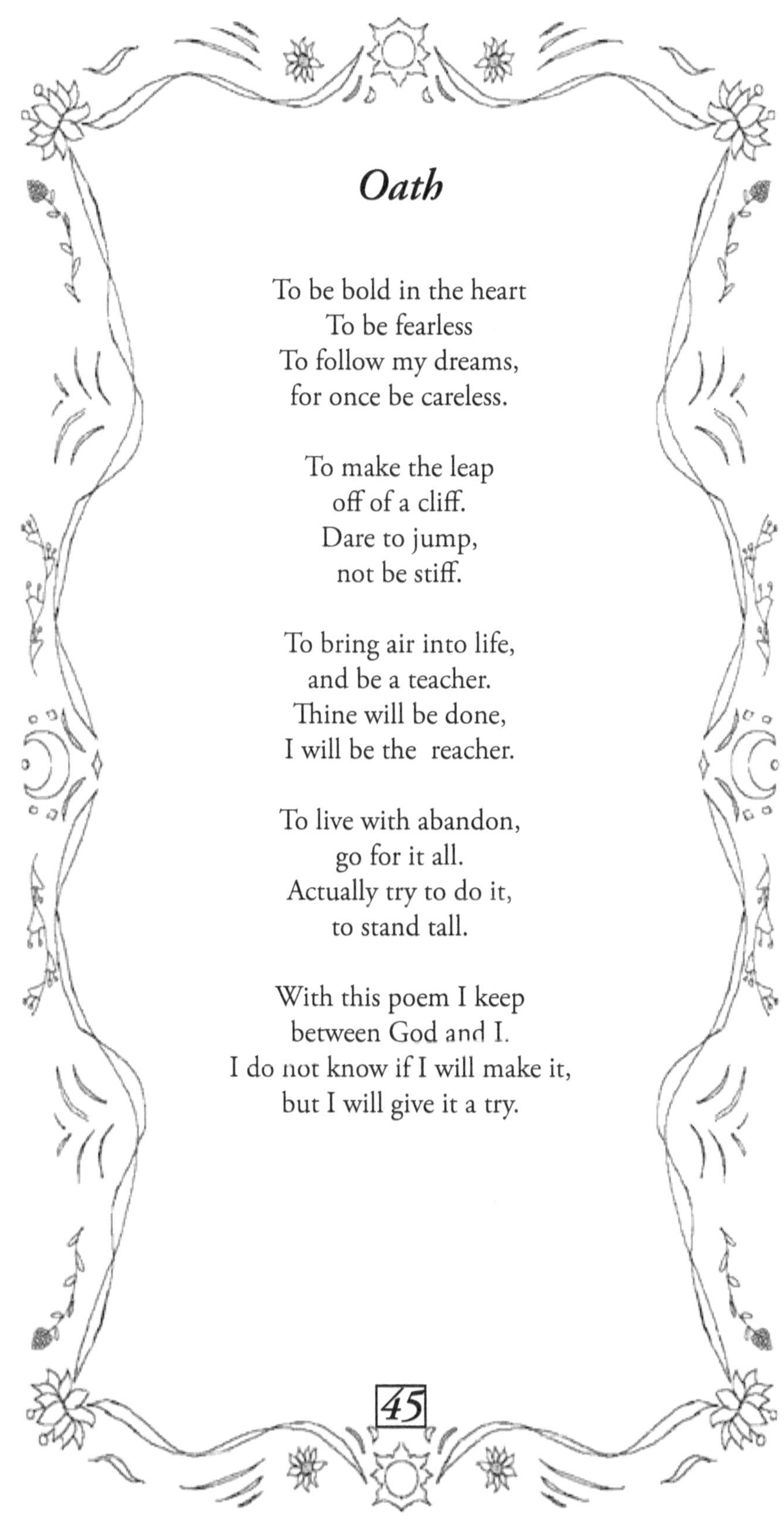

Oath

To be bold in the heart
To be fearless
To follow my dreams,
for once be careless.

To make the leap
off of a cliff.
Dare to jump,
not be stiff.

To bring air into life,
and be a teacher.
Thine will be done,
I will be the reacher.

To live with abandon,
go for it all.
Actually try to do it,
to stand tall.

With this poem I keep
between God and I.
I do not know if I will make it,
but I will give it a try.

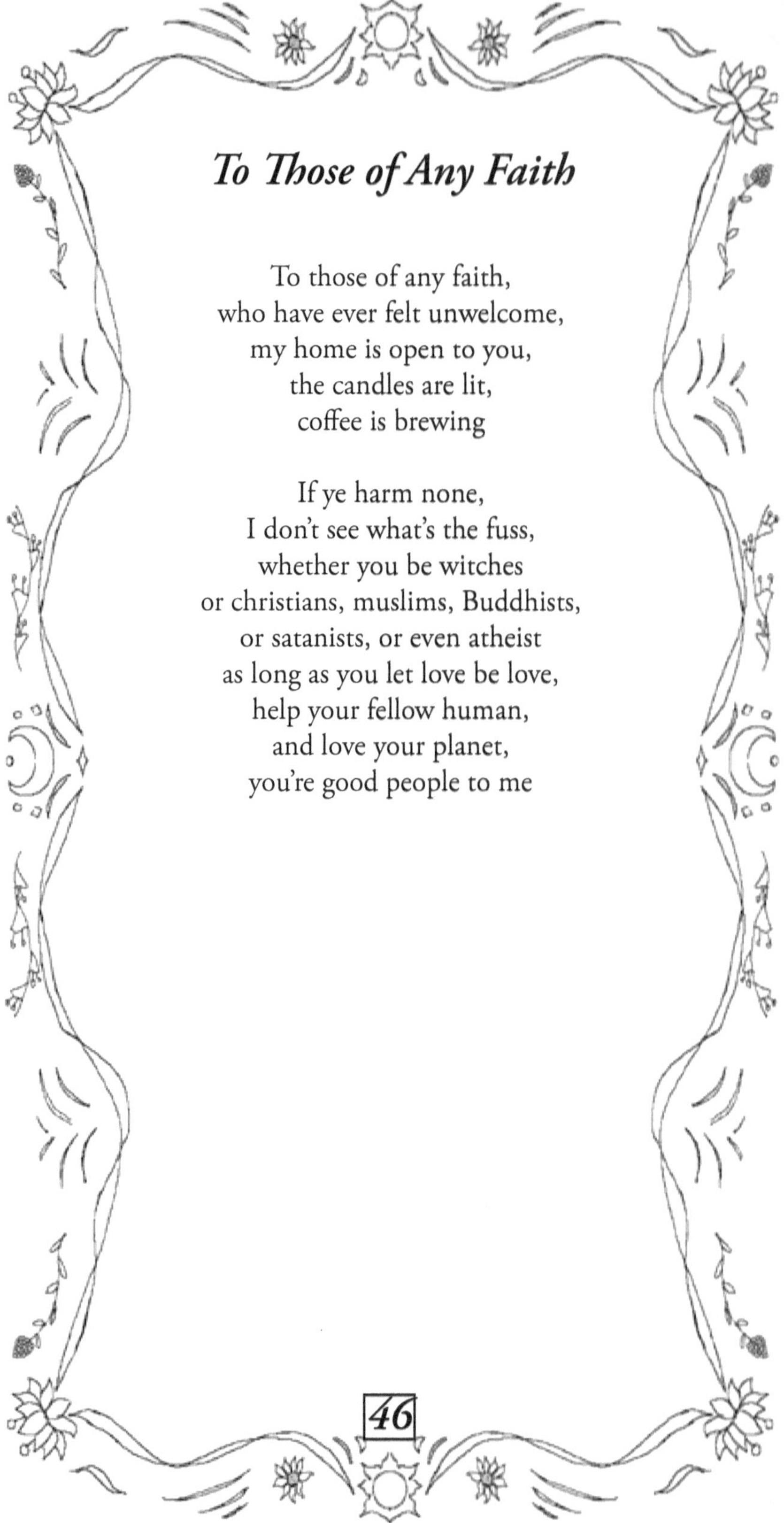

To Those of Any Faith

To those of any faith,
who have ever felt unwelcome,
my home is open to you,
the candles are lit,
coffee is brewing

If ye harm none,
I don't see what's the fuss,
whether you be witches
or christians, muslims, Buddhists,
or satanists, or even atheist
as long as you let love be love,
help your fellow human,
and love your planet,
you're good people to me

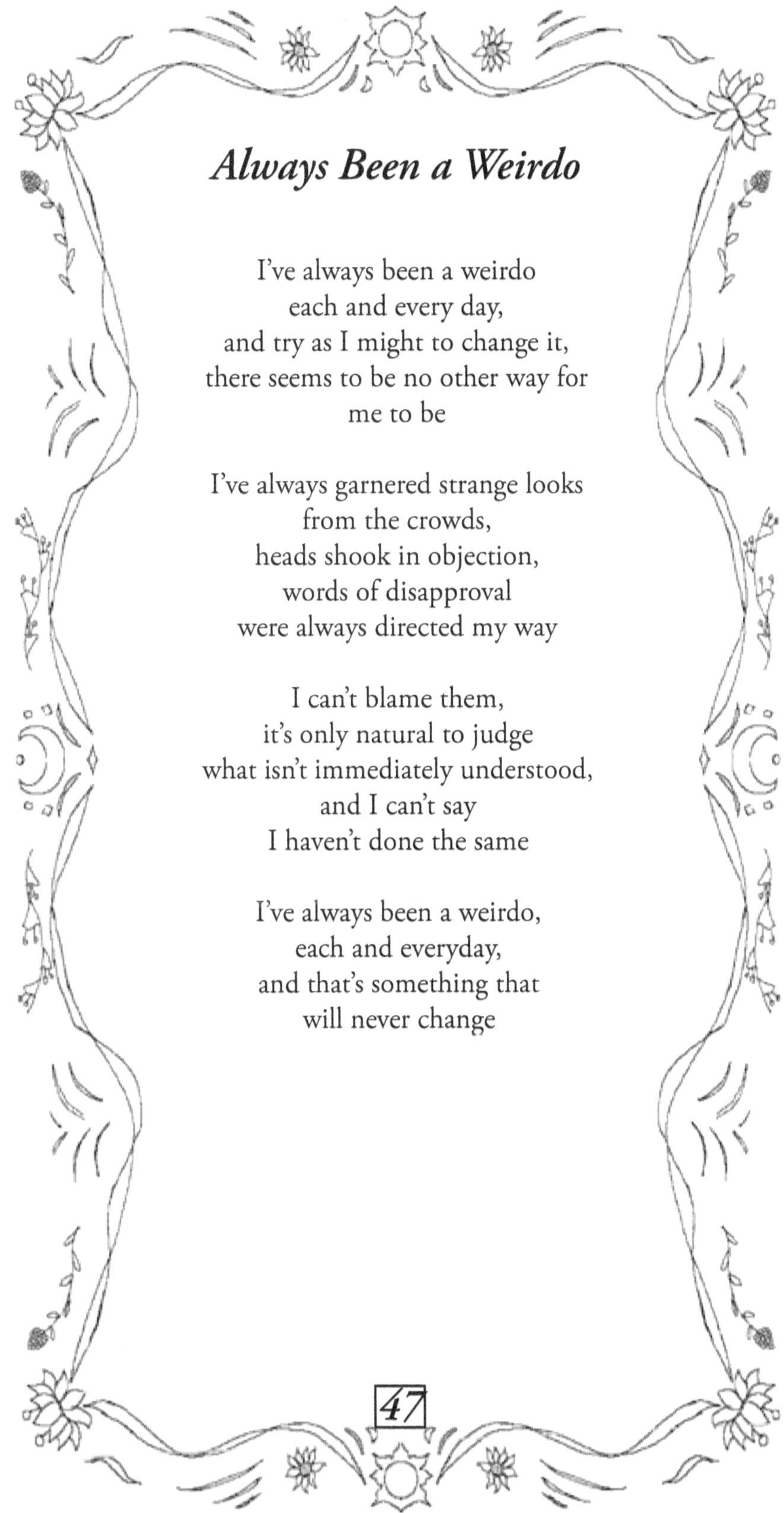

Always Been a Weirdo

I've always been a weirdo
each and every day,
and try as I might to change it,
there seems to be no other way for
me to be

I've always garnered strange looks
from the crowds,
heads shook in objection,
words of disapproval
were always directed my way

I can't blame them,
it's only natural to judge
what isn't immediately understood,
and I can't say
I haven't done the same

I've always been a weirdo,
each and everyday,
and that's something that
will never change

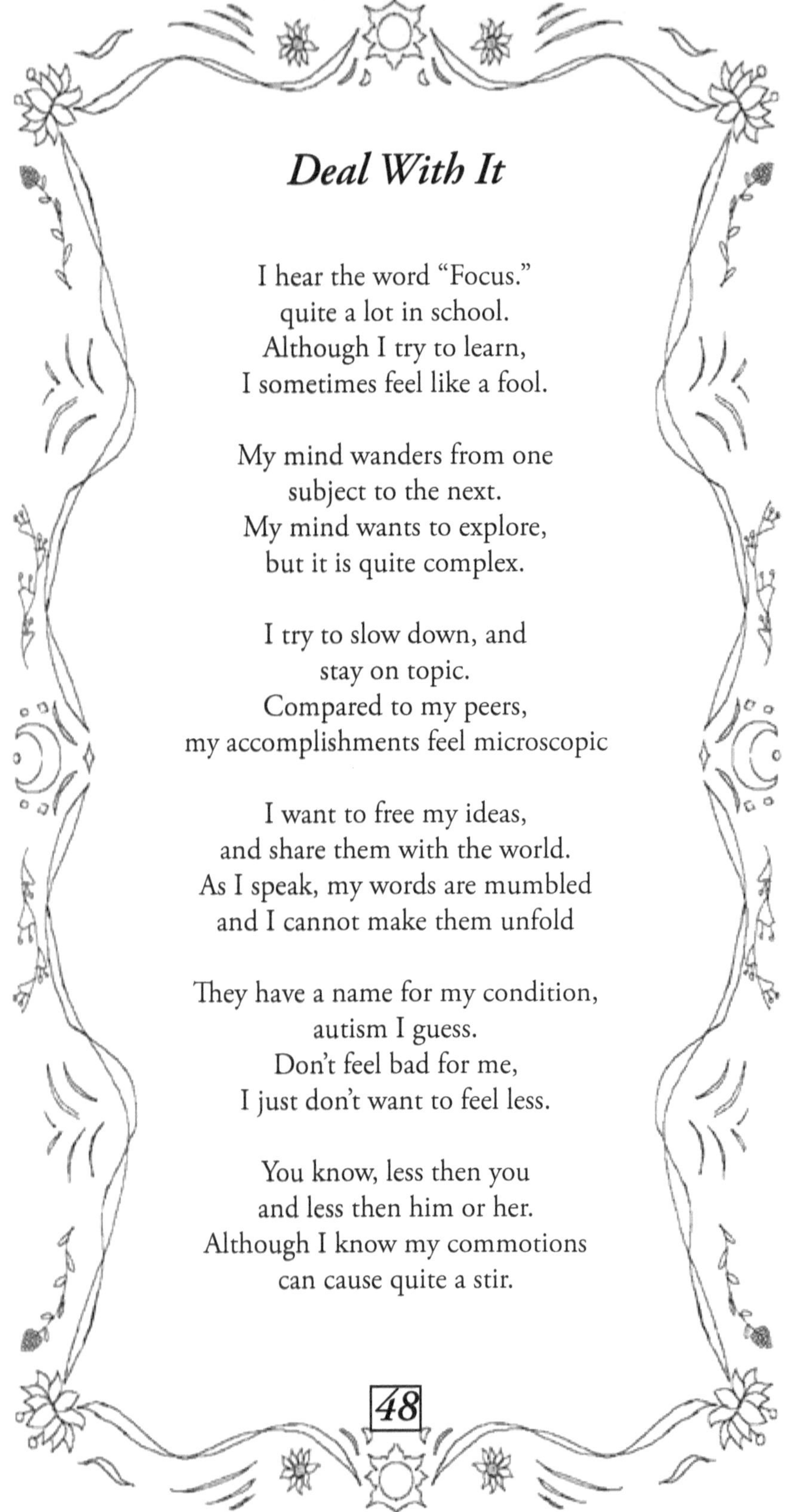

Deal With It

I hear the word "Focus."
quite a lot in school.
Although I try to learn,
I sometimes feel like a fool.

My mind wanders from one
subject to the next.
My mind wants to explore,
but it is quite complex.

I try to slow down, and
stay on topic.
Compared to my peers,
my accomplishments feel microscopic

I want to free my ideas,
and share them with the world.
As I speak, my words are mumbled
and I cannot make them unfold

They have a name for my condition,
autism I guess.
Don't feel bad for me,
I just don't want to feel less.

You know, less then you
and less then him or her.
Although I know my commotions
can cause quite a stir.

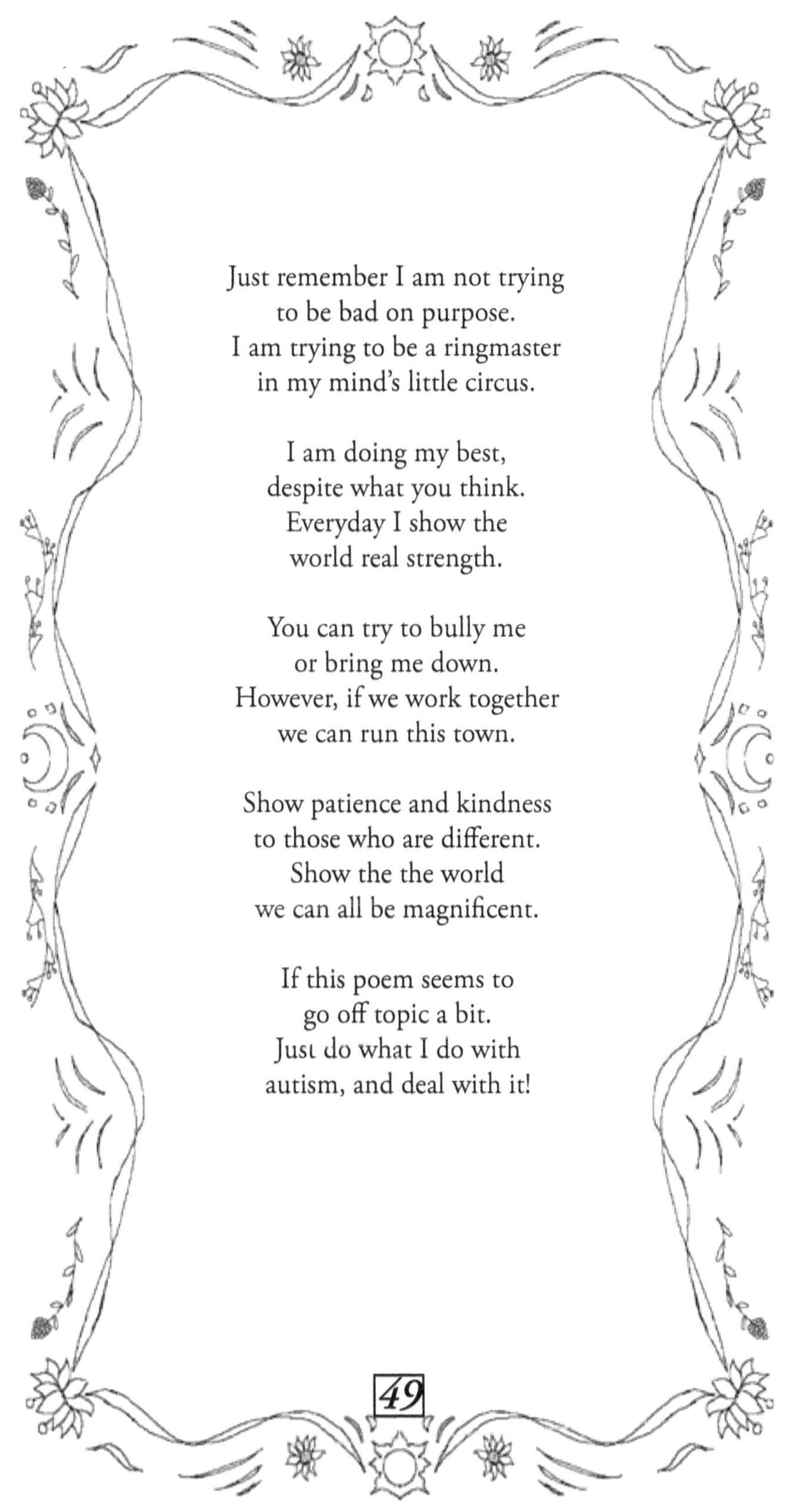

Just remember I am not trying
to be bad on purpose.
I am trying to be a ringmaster
in my mind's little circus.

I am doing my best,
despite what you think.
Everyday I show the
world real strength.

You can try to bully me
or bring me down.
However, if we work together
we can run this town.

Show patience and kindness
to those who are different.
Show the the world
we can all be magnificent.

If this poem seems to
go off topic a bit.
Just do what I do with
autism, and deal with it!

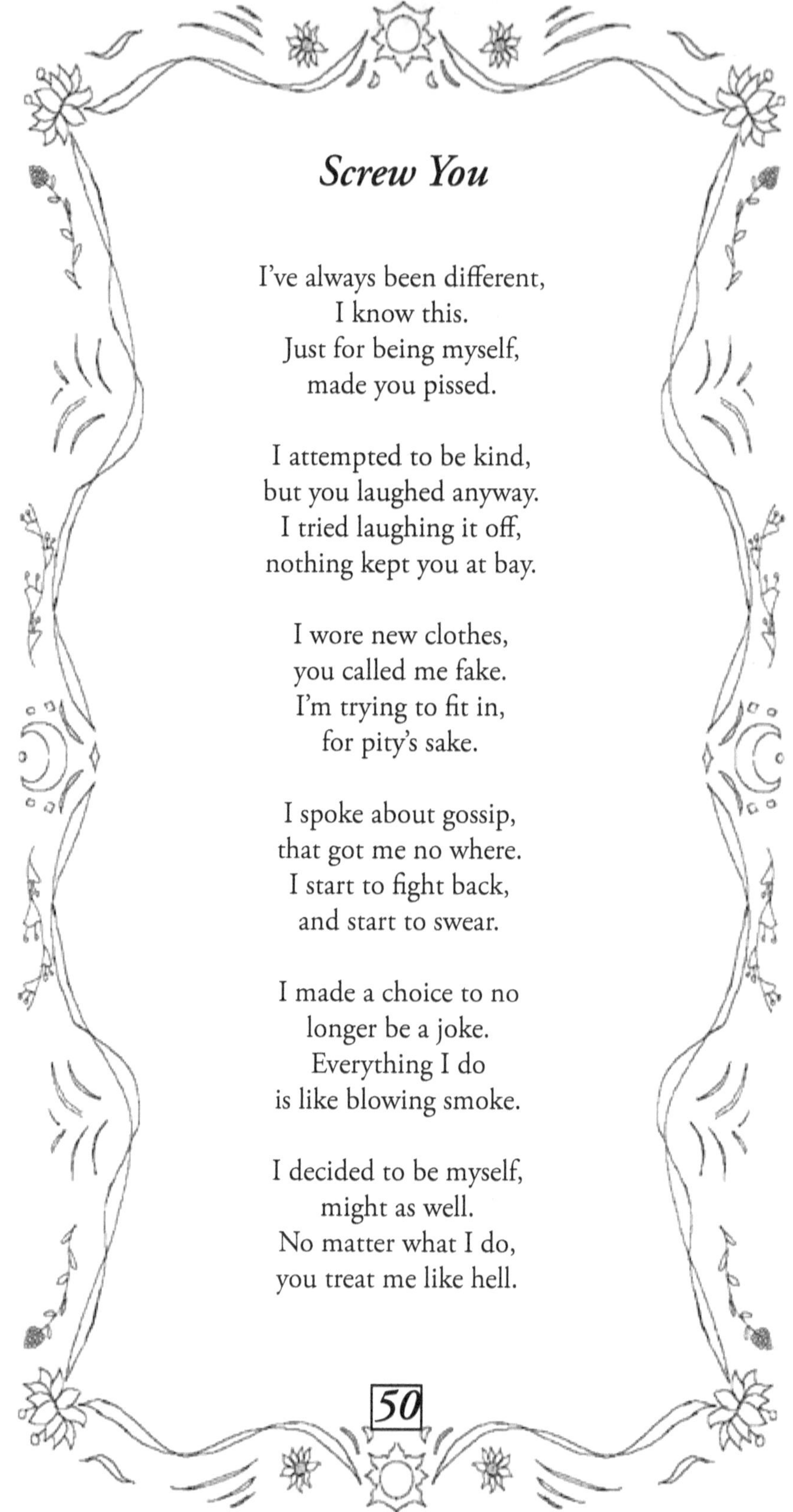

Screw You

I've always been different,
I know this.
Just for being myself,
made you pissed.

I attempted to be kind,
but you laughed anyway.
I tried laughing it off,
nothing kept you at bay.

I wore new clothes,
you called me fake.
I'm trying to fit in,
for pity's sake.

I spoke about gossip,
that got me no where.
I start to fight back,
and start to swear.

I made a choice to no
longer be a joke.
Everything I do
is like blowing smoke.

I decided to be myself,
might as well.
No matter what I do,
you treat me like hell.

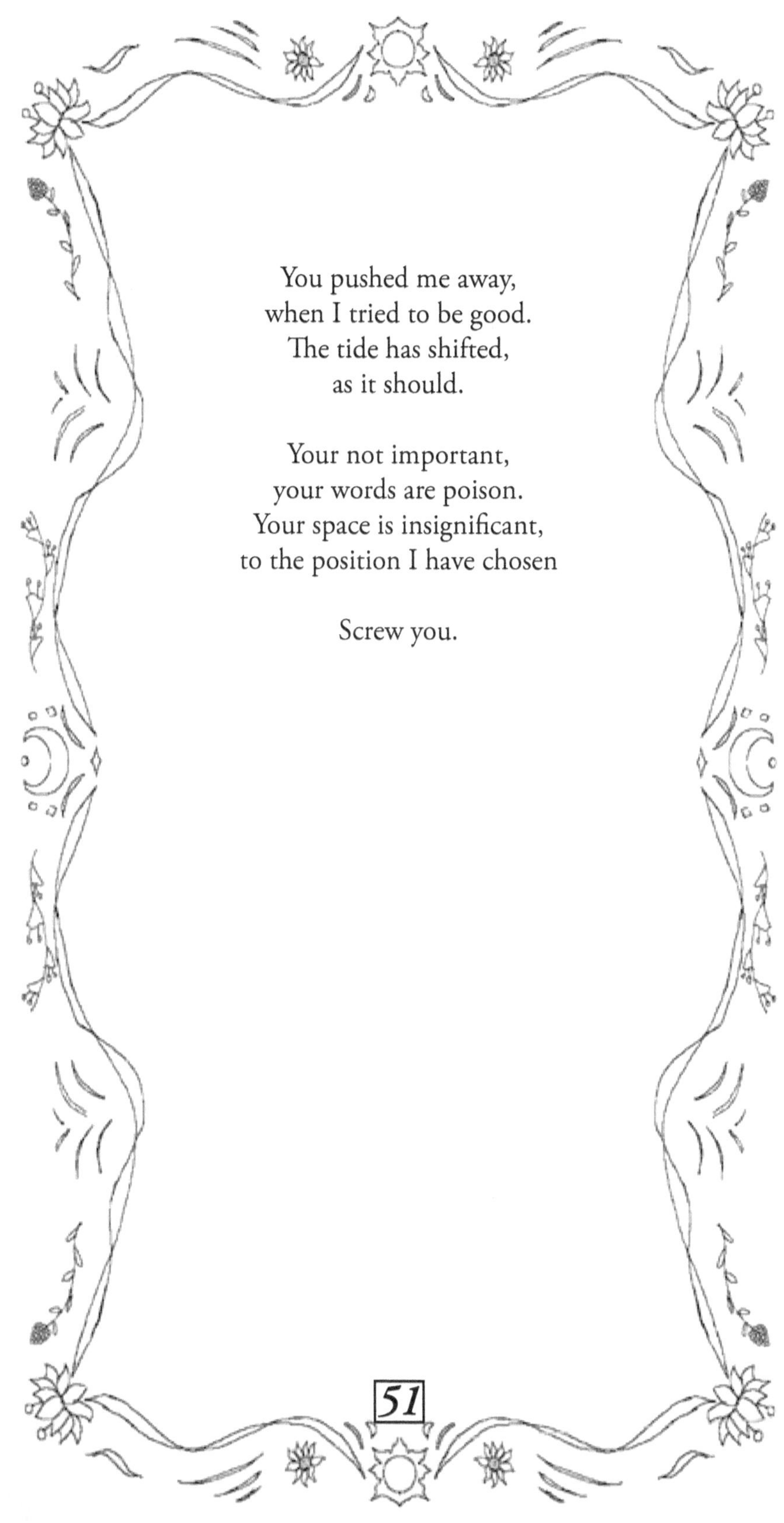

You pushed me away,
when I tried to be good.
The tide has shifted,
as it should.

Your not important,
your words are poison.
Your space is insignificant,
to the position I have chosen

Screw you.

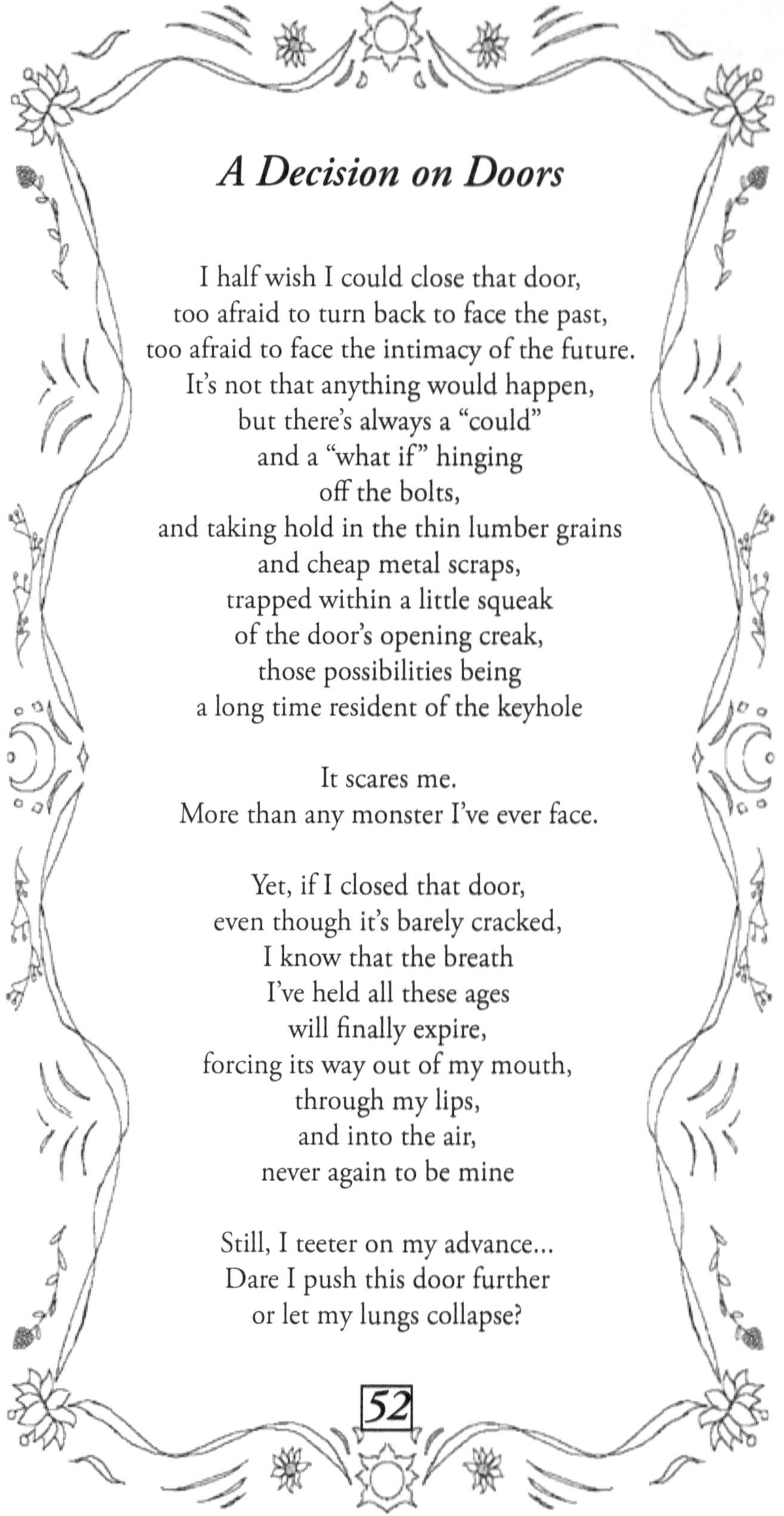

A Decision on Doors

I half wish I could close that door,
too afraid to turn back to face the past,
too afraid to face the intimacy of the future.
It's not that anything would happen,
but there's always a "could"
and a "what if" hinging
off the bolts,
and taking hold in the thin lumber grains
and cheap metal scraps,
trapped within a little squeak
of the door's opening creak,
those possibilities being
a long time resident of the keyhole

It scares me.
More than any monster I've ever face.

Yet, if I closed that door,
even though it's barely cracked,
I know that the breath
I've held all these ages
will finally expire,
forcing its way out of my mouth,
through my lips,
and into the air,
never again to be mine

Still, I teeter on my advance...
Dare I push this door further
or let my lungs collapse?

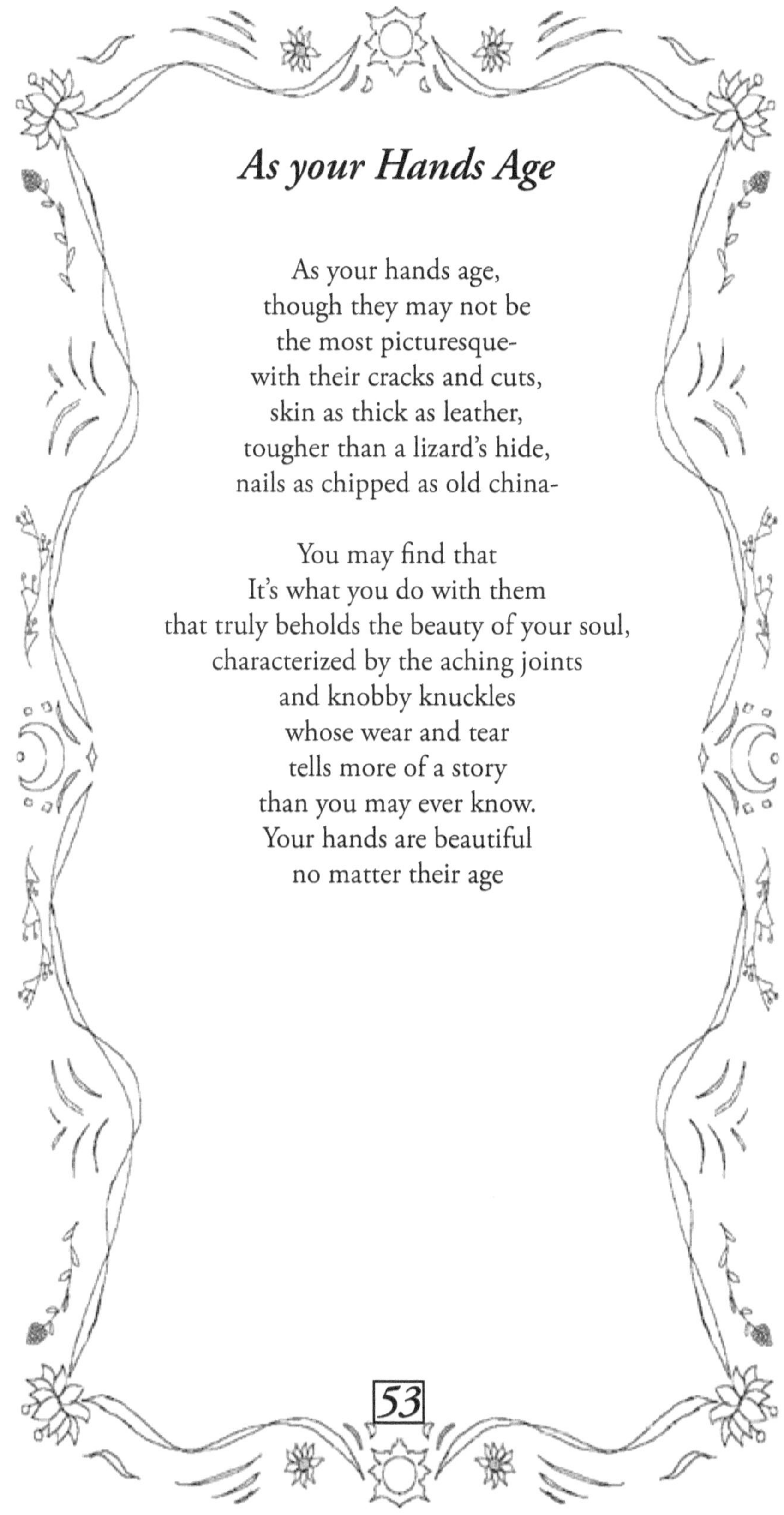

As your Hands Age

As your hands age,
though they may not be
the most picturesque-
with their cracks and cuts,
skin as thick as leather,
tougher than a lizard's hide,
nails as chipped as old china-

You may find that
It's what you do with them
that truly beholds the beauty of your soul,
characterized by the aching joints
and knobby knuckles
whose wear and tear
tells more of a story
than you may ever know.
Your hands are beautiful
no matter their age

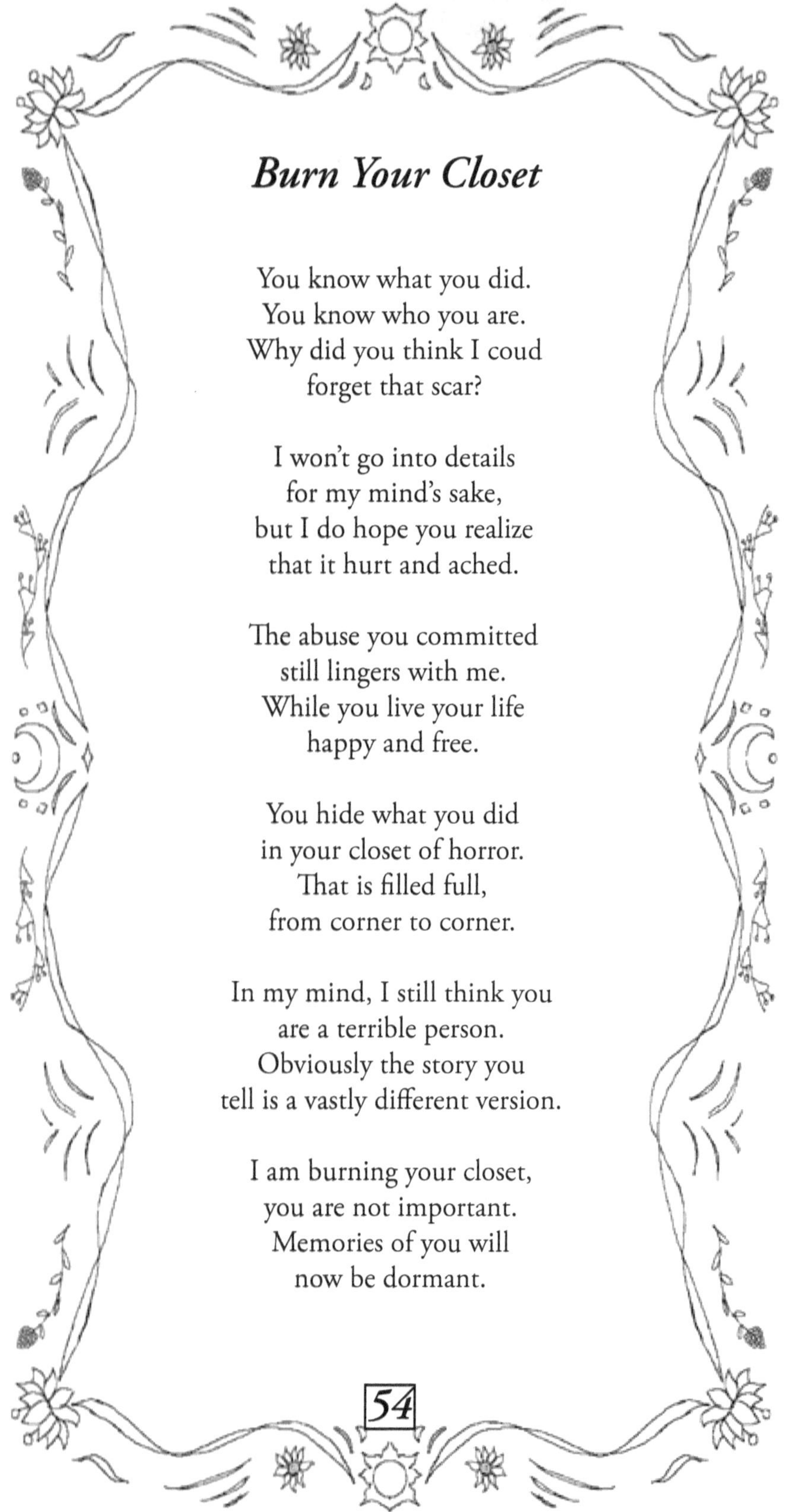

Burn Your Closet

You know what you did.
You know who you are.
Why did you think I coud
forget that scar?

I won't go into details
for my mind's sake,
but I do hope you realize
that it hurt and ached.

The abuse you committed
still lingers with me.
While you live your life
happy and free.

You hide what you did
in your closet of horror.
That is filled full,
from corner to corner.

In my mind, I still think you
are a terrible person.
Obviously the story you
tell is a vastly different version.

I am burning your closet,
you are not important.
Memories of you will
now be dormant.

I have forgiven myself,
and the decisions I made.
All is now well,
I am no longer afraid.

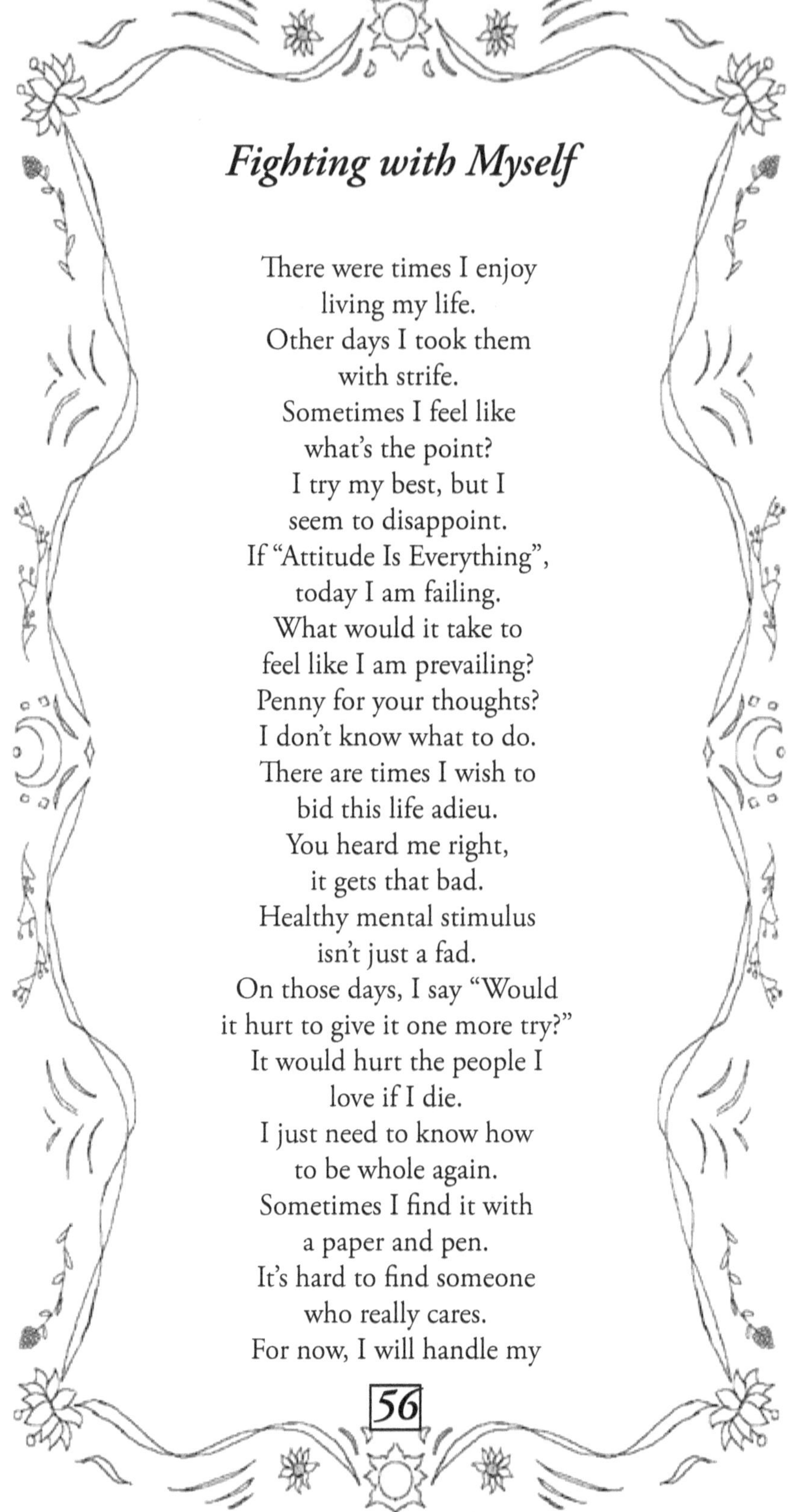

Fighting with Myself

There were times I enjoy
living my life.
Other days I took them
with strife.
Sometimes I feel like
what's the point?
I try my best, but I
seem to disappoint.
If "Attitude Is Everything",
today I am failing.
What would it take to
feel like I am prevailing?
Penny for your thoughts?
I don't know what to do.
There are times I wish to
bid this life adieu.
You heard me right,
it gets that bad.
Healthy mental stimulus
isn't just a fad.
On those days, I say "Would
it hurt to give it one more try?"
It would hurt the people I
love if I die.
I just need to know how
to be whole again.
Sometimes I find it with
a paper and pen.
It's hard to find someone
who really cares.
For now, I will handle my

own affairs.
Depression and anxiety
sucks guys.
You don't what goes on
underneath my guise.

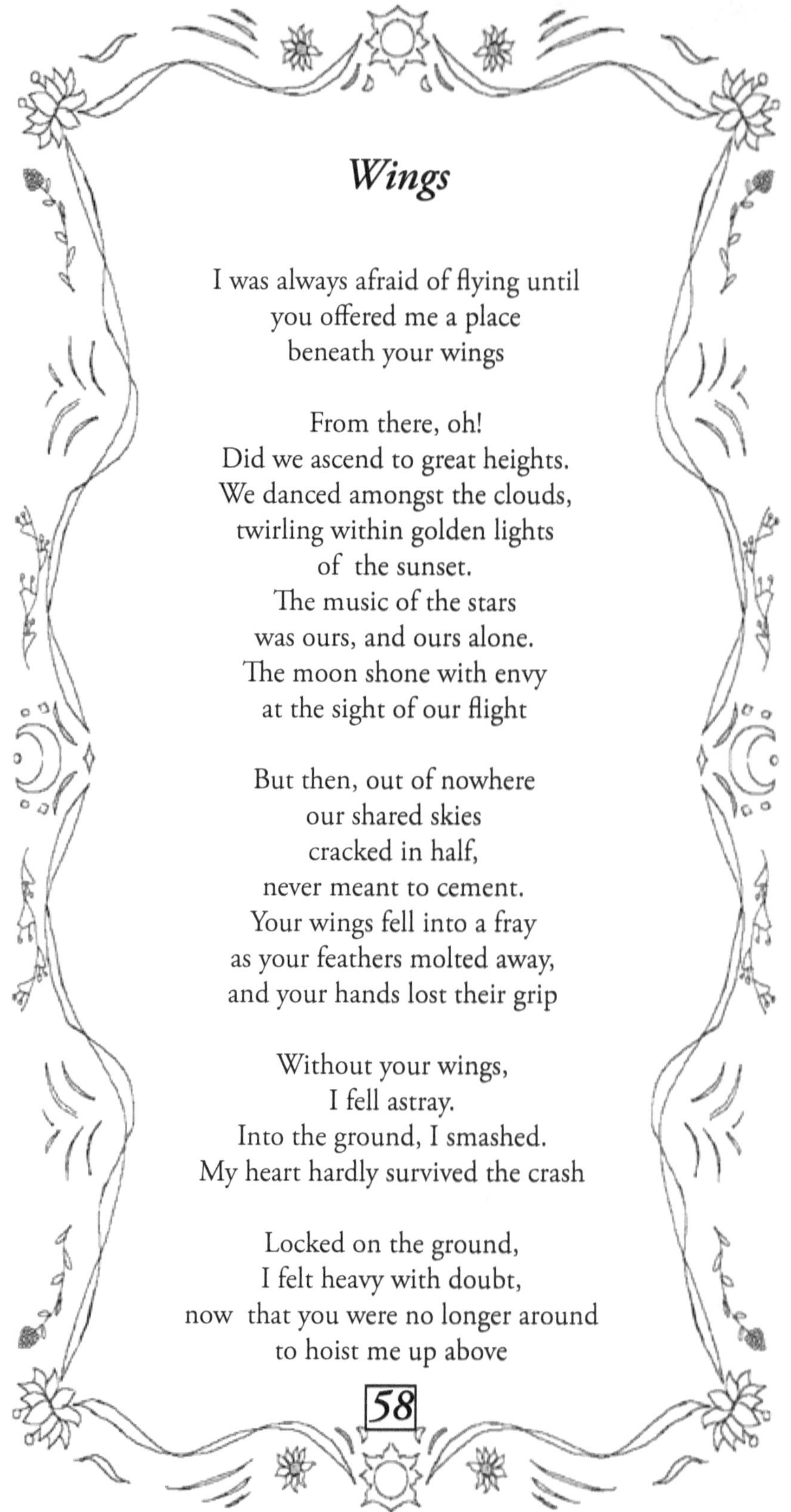

Wings

I was always afraid of flying until
you offered me a place
beneath your wings

From there, oh!
Did we ascend to great heights.
We danced amongst the clouds,
twirling within golden lights
of the sunset.
The music of the stars
was ours, and ours alone.
The moon shone with envy
at the sight of our flight

But then, out of nowhere
our shared skies
cracked in half,
never meant to cement.
Your wings fell into a fray
as your feathers molted away,
and your hands lost their grip

Without your wings,
I fell astray.
Into the ground, I smashed.
My heart hardly survived the crash

Locked on the ground,
I felt heavy with doubt,
now that you were no longer around
to hoist me up above

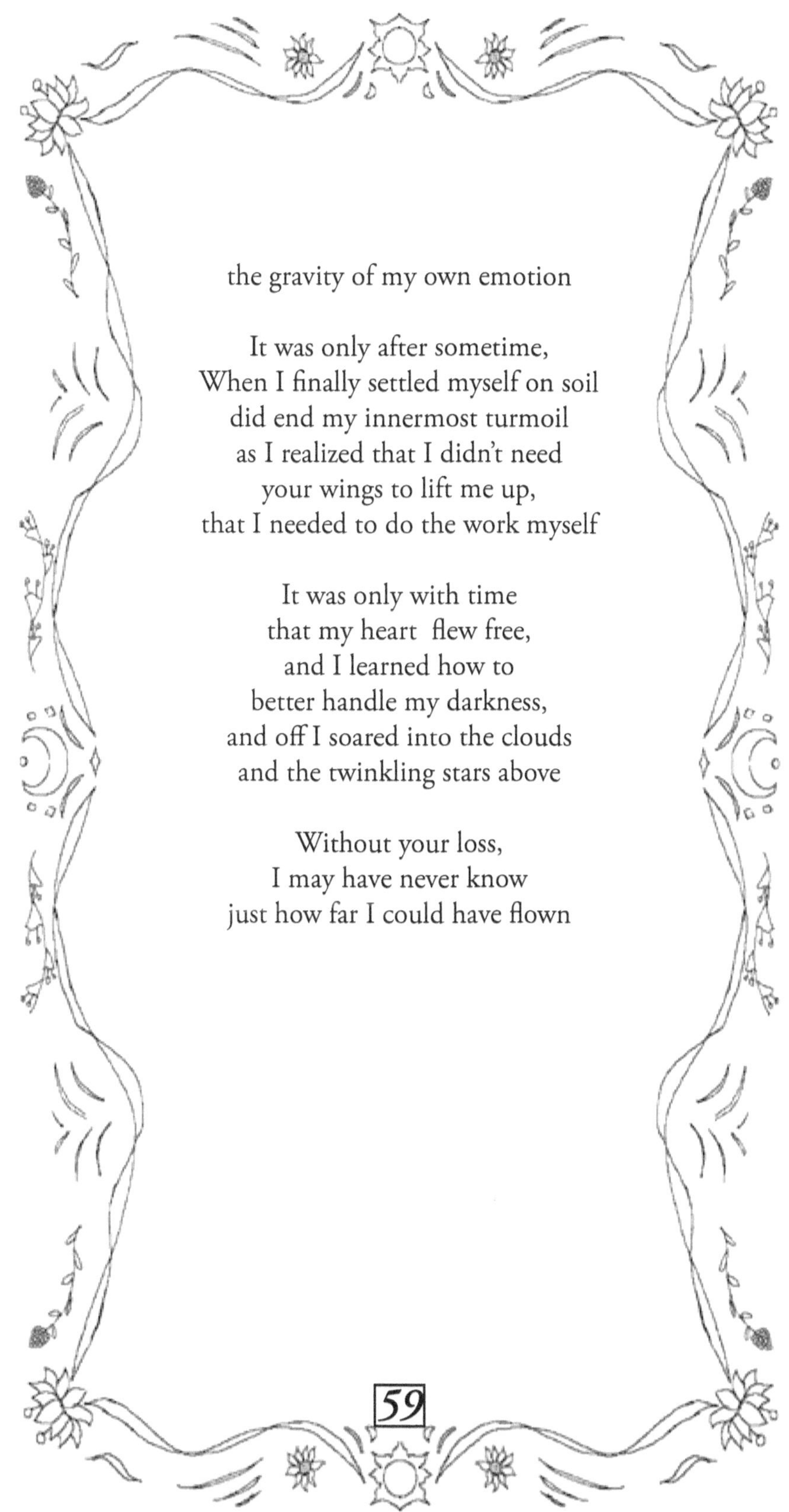

the gravity of my own emotion

It was only after sometime,
When I finally settled myself on soil
did end my innermost turmoil
as I realized that I didn't need
your wings to lift me up,
that I needed to do the work myself

It was only with time
that my heart flew free,
and I learned how to
better handle my darkness,
and off I soared into the clouds
and the twinkling stars above

Without your loss,
I may have never know
just how far I could have flown

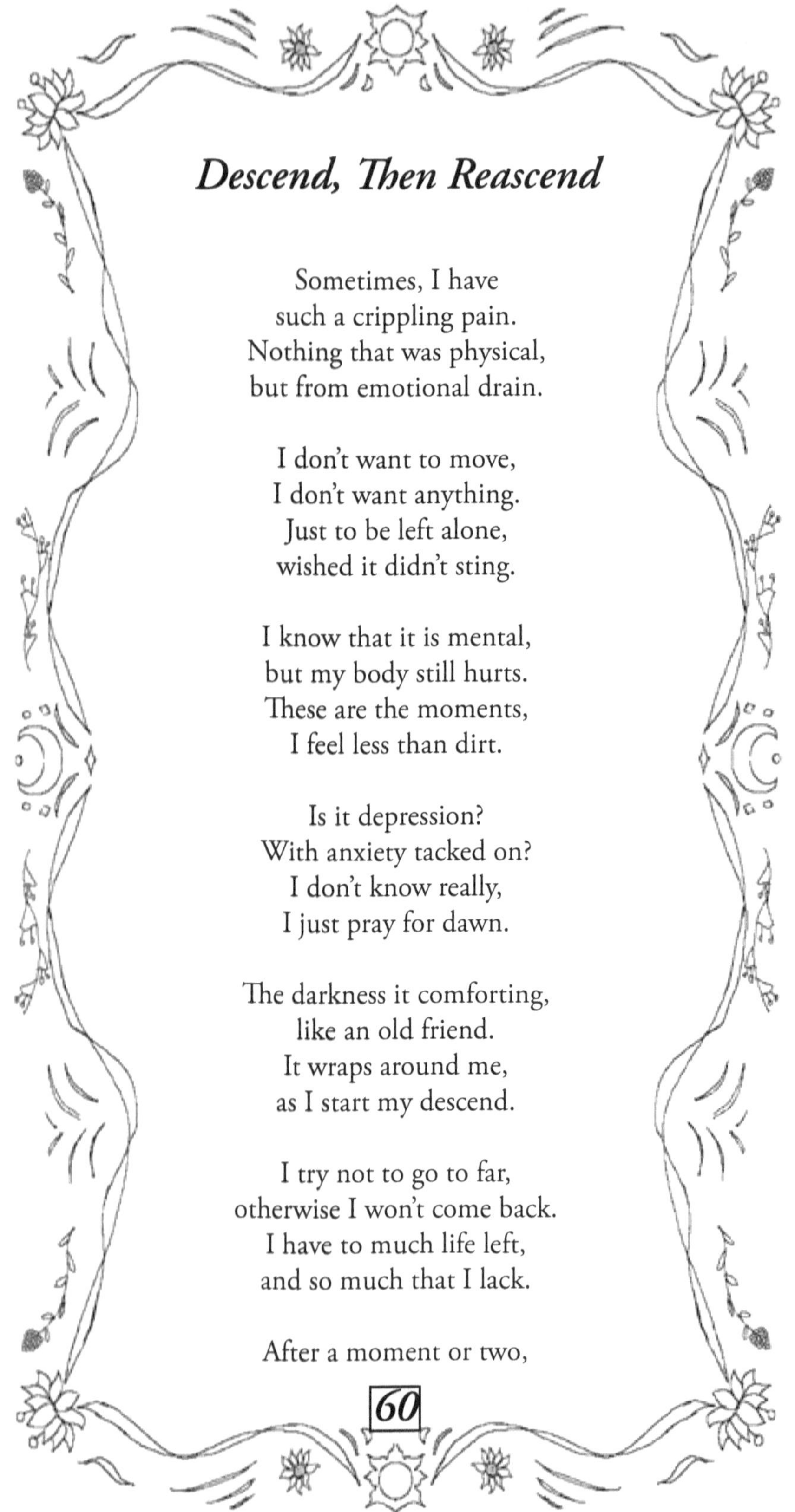

Descend, Then Reascend

Sometimes, I have
such a crippling pain.
Nothing that was physical,
but from emotional drain.

I don't want to move,
I don't want anything.
Just to be left alone,
wished it didn't sting.

I know that it is mental,
but my body still hurts.
These are the moments,
I feel less than dirt.

Is it depression?
With anxiety tacked on?
I don't know really,
I just pray for dawn.

The darkness it comforting,
like an old friend.
It wraps around me,
as I start my descend.

I try not to go to far,
otherwise I won't come back.
I have to much life left,
and so much that I lack.

After a moment or two,

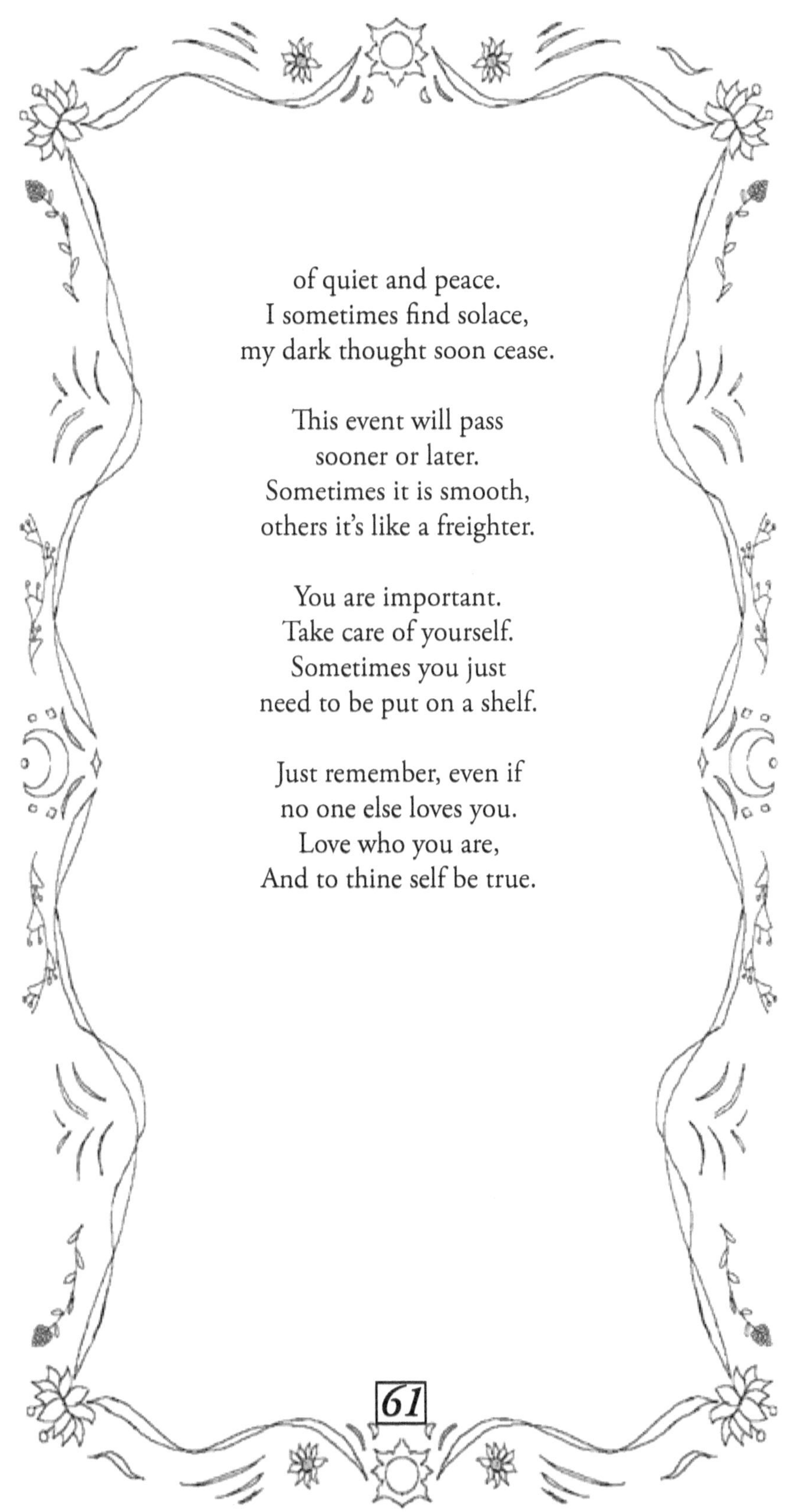

of quiet and peace.
I sometimes find solace,
my dark thought soon cease.

This event will pass
sooner or later.
Sometimes it is smooth,
others it's like a freighter.

You are important.
Take care of yourself.
Sometimes you just
need to be put on a shelf.

Just remember, even if
no one else loves you.
Love who you are,
And to thine self be true.

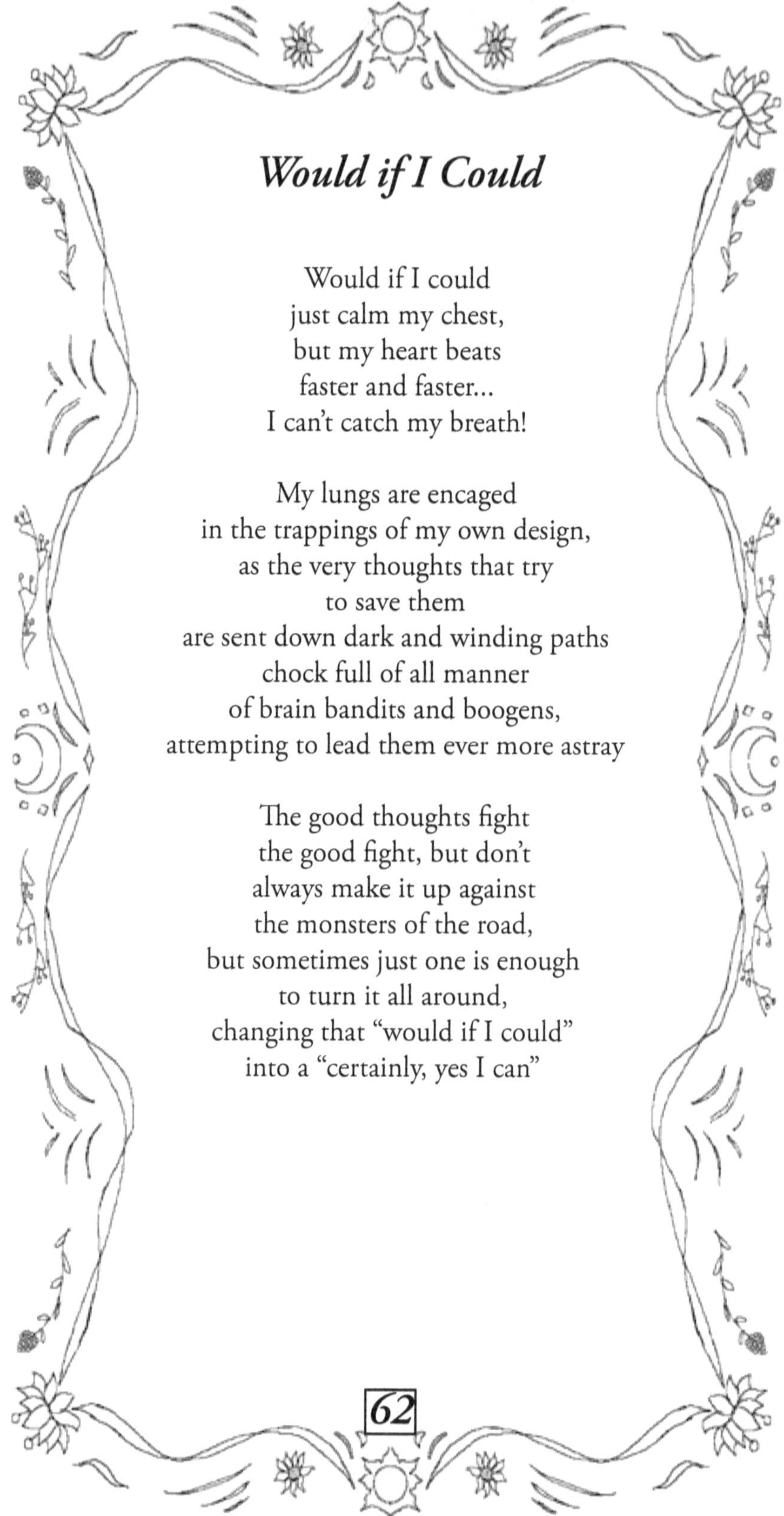

Would if I Could

Would if I could
just calm my chest,
but my heart beats
faster and faster...
I can't catch my breath!

My lungs are encaged
in the trappings of my own design,
as the very thoughts that try
to save them
are sent down dark and winding paths
chock full of all manner
of brain bandits and boogens,
attempting to lead them ever more astray

The good thoughts fight
the good fight, but don't
always make it up against
the monsters of the road,
but sometimes just one is enough
to turn it all around,
changing that "would if I could"
into a "certainly, yes I can"

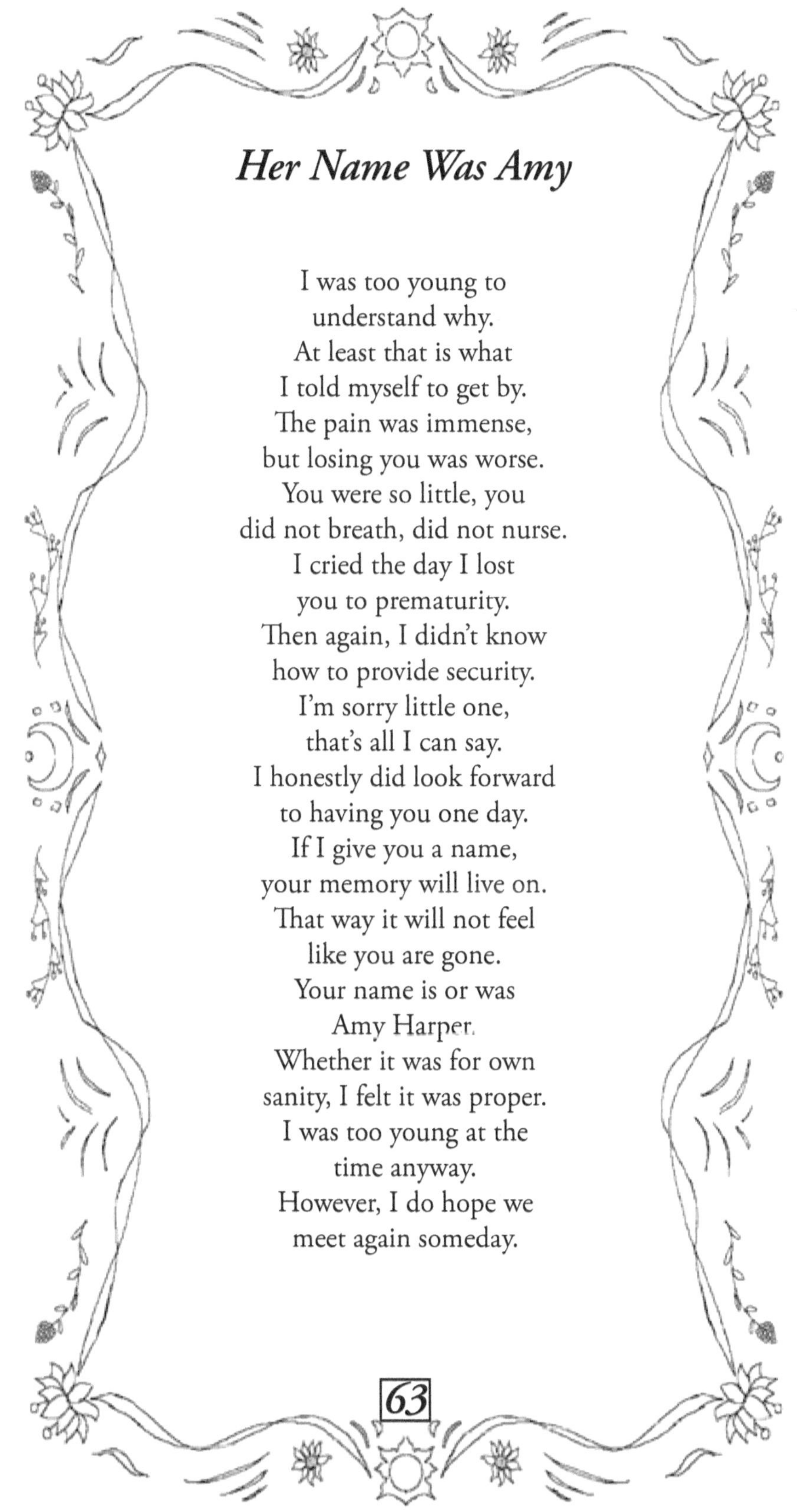

Her Name Was Amy

I was too young to
understand why.
At least that is what
I told myself to get by.
The pain was immense,
but losing you was worse.
You were so little, you
did not breath, did not nurse.
I cried the day I lost
you to prematurity.
Then again, I didn't know
how to provide security.
I'm sorry little one,
that's all I can say.
I honestly did look forward
to having you one day.
If I give you a name,
your memory will live on.
That way it will not feel
like you are gone.
Your name is or was
Amy Harper.
Whether it was for own
sanity, I felt it was proper.
I was too young at the
time anyway.
However, I do hope we
meet again someday.

Odds and Ends

Poems of Uncategorized Fun

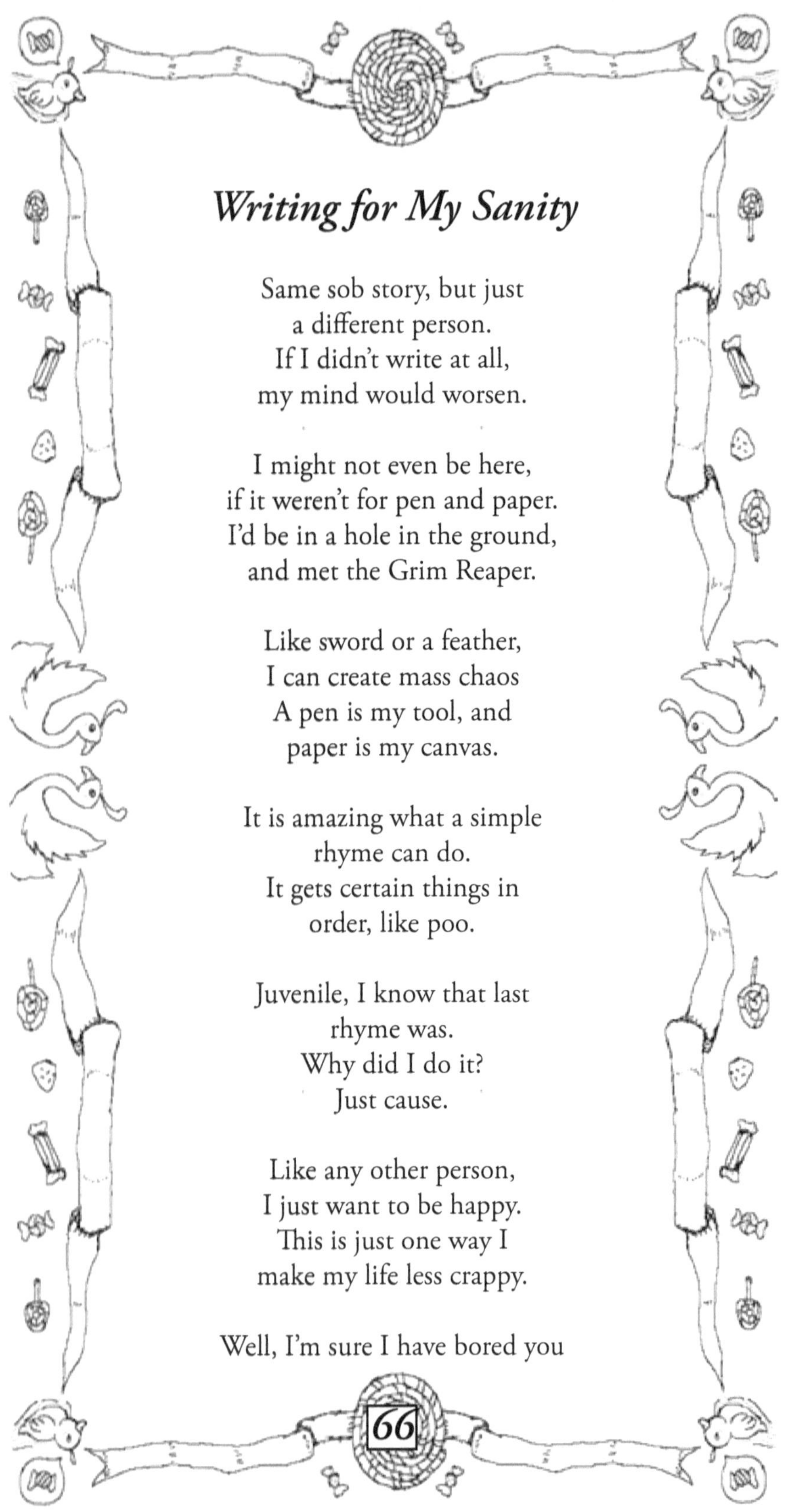

Writing for My Sanity

Same sob story, but just
a different person.
If I didn't write at all,
my mind would worsen.

I might not even be here,
if it weren't for pen and paper.
I'd be in a hole in the ground,
and met the Grim Reaper.

Like sword or a feather,
I can create mass chaos
A pen is my tool, and
paper is my canvas.

It is amazing what a simple
rhyme can do.
It gets certain things in
order, like poo.

Juvenile, I know that last
rhyme was.
Why did I do it?
Just cause.

Like any other person,
I just want to be happy.
This is just one way I
make my life less crappy.

Well, I'm sure I have bored you

enough today.
Really this poem has nothing
great to say.

Just keep writing, even
if it doesn't make sense.
Whether it is short, or
full of suspense.

Believe me, it is not
for the vanity.
Sometimes, you write
just to keep your sanity.

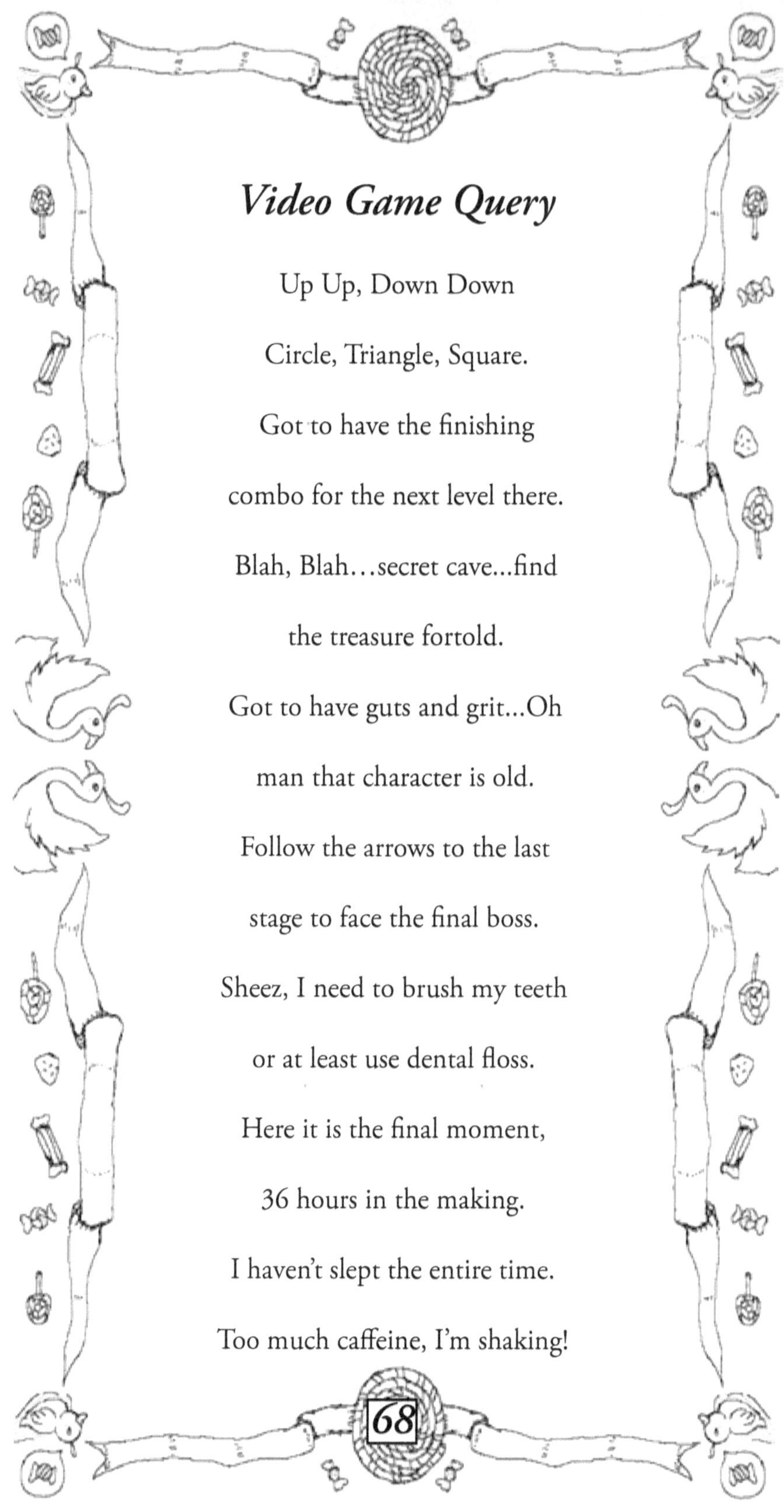

Video Game Query

Up Up, Down Down

Circle, Triangle, Square.

Got to have the finishing

combo for the next level there.

Blah, Blah…secret cave…find

the treasure fortold.

Got to have guts and grit…Oh

man that character is old.

Follow the arrows to the last

stage to face the final boss.

Sheez, I need to brush my teeth

or at least use dental floss.

Here it is the final moment,

36 hours in the making.

I haven't slept the entire time.

Too much caffeine, I'm shaking!

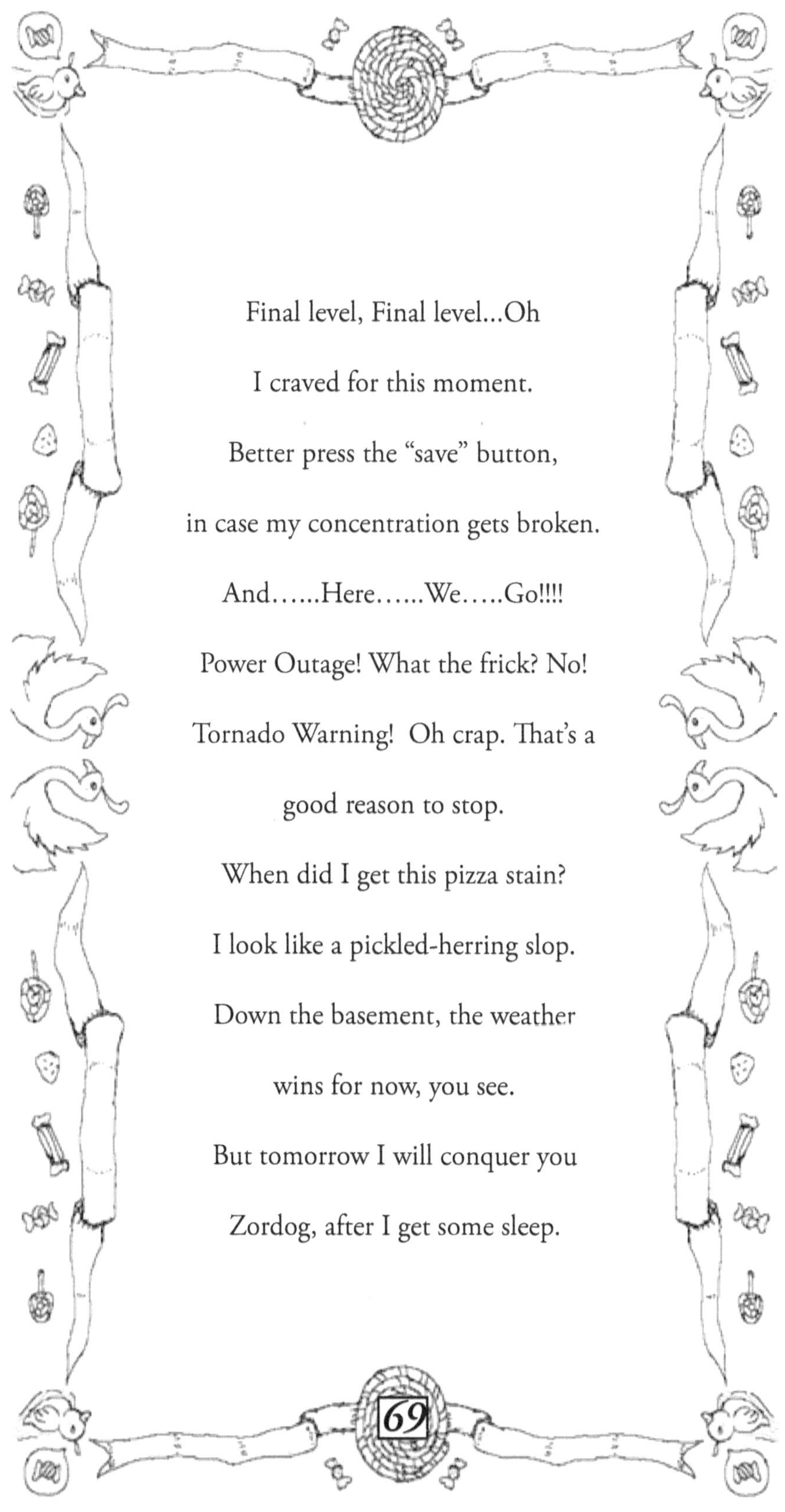

Final level, Final level...Oh

I craved for this moment.

Better press the "save" button,

in case my concentration gets broken.

And…...Here…...We…..Go!!!!

Power Outage! What the frick? No!

Tornado Warning! Oh crap. That's a

good reason to stop.

When did I get this pizza stain?

I look like a pickled-herring slop.

Down the basement, the weather

wins for now, you see.

But tomorrow I will conquer you

Zordog, after I get some sleep.

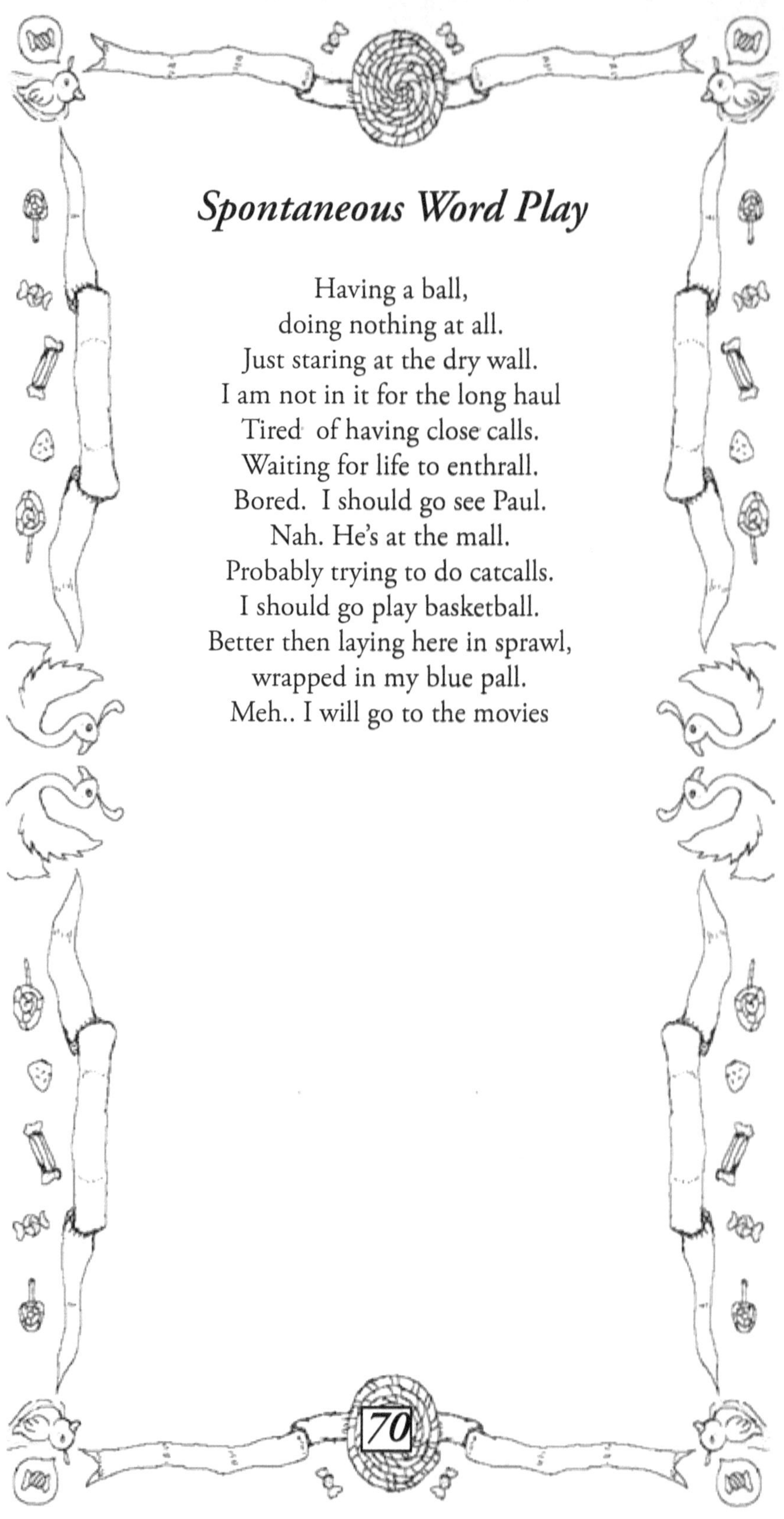

Spontaneous Word Play

Having a ball,
doing nothing at all.
Just staring at the dry wall.
I am not in it for the long haul
Tired of having close calls.
Waiting for life to enthrall.
Bored. I should go see Paul.
Nah. He's at the mall.
Probably trying to do catcalls.
I should go play basketball.
Better then laying here in sprawl,
wrapped in my blue pall.
Meh.. I will go to the movies

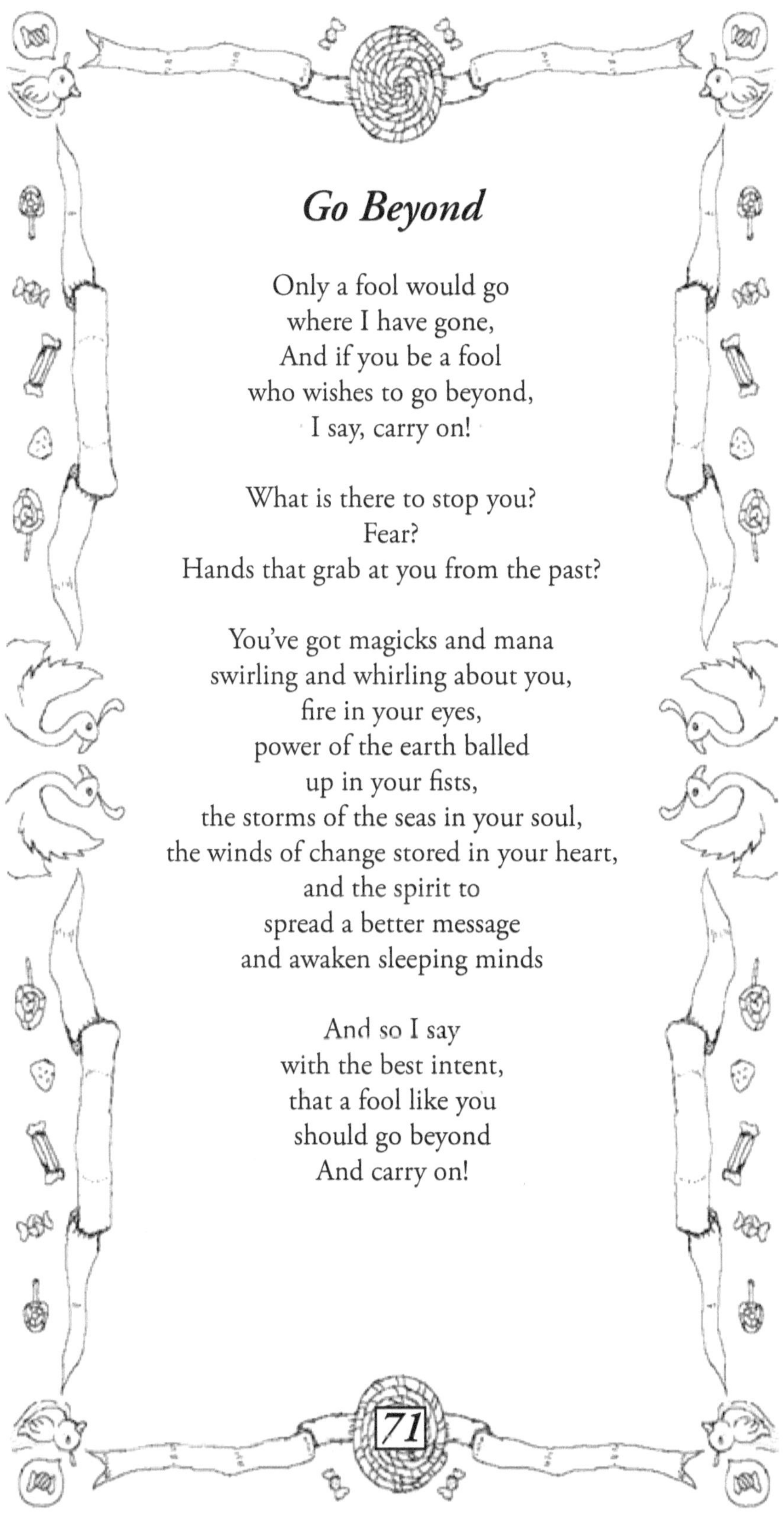

Go Beyond

Only a fool would go
where I have gone,
And if you be a fool
who wishes to go beyond,
I say, carry on!

What is there to stop you?
Fear?
Hands that grab at you from the past?

You've got magicks and mana
swirling and whirling about you,
fire in your eyes,
power of the earth balled
up in your fists,
the storms of the seas in your soul,
the winds of change stored in your heart,
and the spirit to
spread a better message
and awaken sleeping minds

And so I say
with the best intent,
that a fool like you
should go beyond
And carry on!

Happy Place, Empty Space

"You're fat."
Good golly!
"You're dumb."
Hot Tamale!
"You're ugly."
Fools folly!
"You're nothing."
California trolley!
"You're weird."
Pocket Polly!
"What?"
Border Collie!
"Stop it!"
Holly Jolly!
"This is idiotic!"
Pop Lolly!
"This makes no sense!"
Critter Crawly!
"Quit Moron!"
Little Dolly!
"Walking away now!"
Thank you for playing.

Chocolate!

Sweet, lovely
tasty, sweet.
I said it twice,
Worth the repeat.

You make my day
better as a treat.
Like a whisper of
love as I eat.

Whether you are
frozen or melted.
With you chocolate,
I am easily tempted.

I savor your last
bite like a tender kiss.
Your taste afterwards
I will dearly miss.

Like all good things,
too much of you is bad.
But the time we share
together makes me glad.

CHOCOLATE!

Randy the Candy Loving Duck

There once was a little duck,
who had dreams, but little luck
He dreamed of sugary delights
and sweets galore
He was named Randy,
and craved only candy,
nothing more

His family never understood
this strange obsession,
and sometimes thought
he was under possession
of a demon who craved
bonbons and fondant

They tried to starve the
want right out of him,
never gave into his whim,
but boy, they sure did spoil Randy,
telling him he ought to feel dandy,
eating the finest fish the pond
had to offer

And though this little duck
was very grateful,
There was just something
that made him unable
to take in the flavor
his parents wished him to savor
"When I grow up", he promised himself
"I'll find a place of my own,

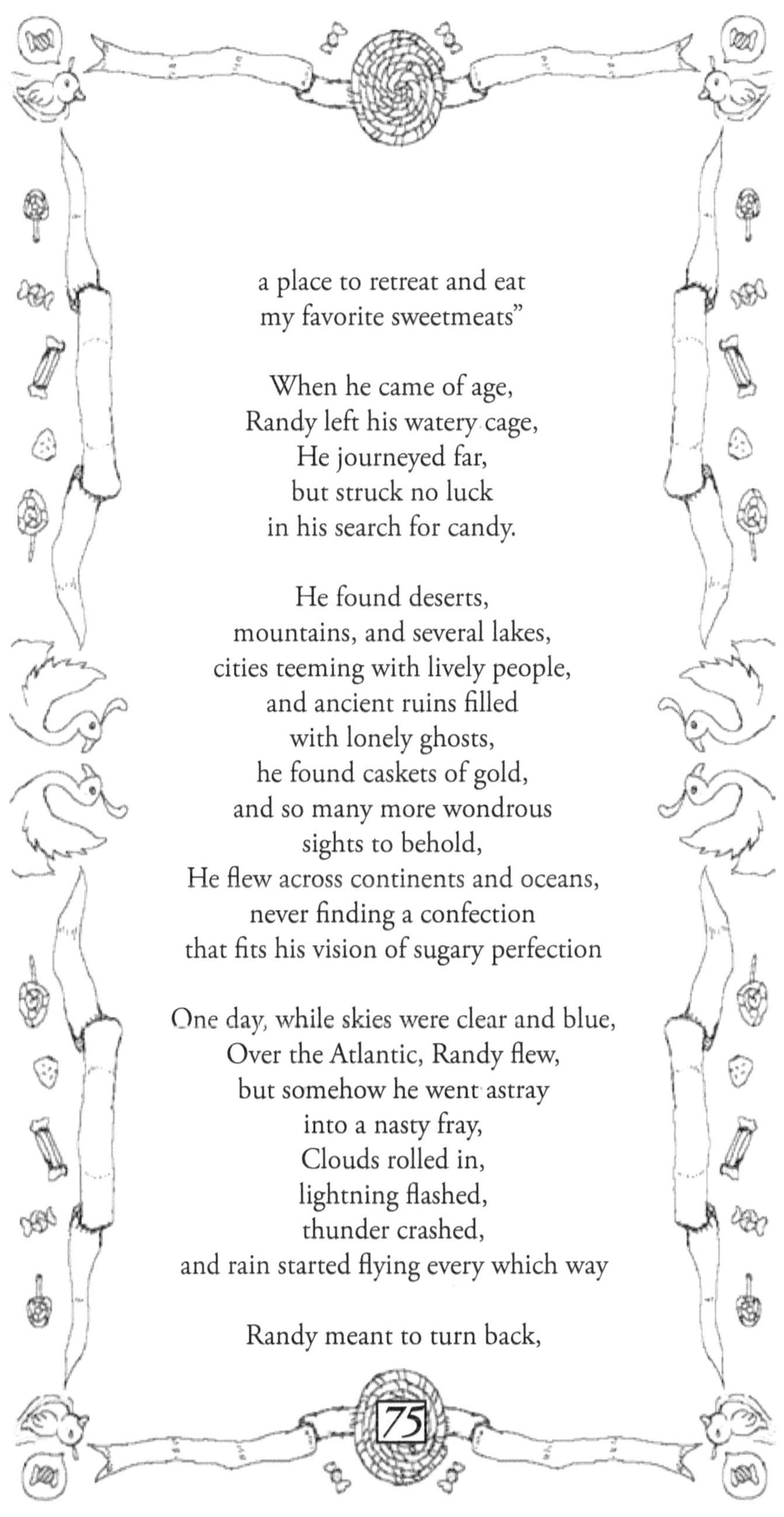

a place to retreat and eat
my favorite sweetmeats"

When he came of age,
Randy left his watery cage,
He journeyed far,
but struck no luck
in his search for candy.

He found deserts,
mountains, and several lakes,
cities teeming with lively people,
and ancient ruins filled
with lonely ghosts,
he found caskets of gold,
and so many more wondrous
sights to behold,
He flew across continents and oceans,
never finding a confection
that fits his vision of sugary perfection

One day, while skies were clear and blue,
Over the Atlantic, Randy flew,
but somehow he went astray
into a nasty fray,
Clouds rolled in,
lightning flashed,
thunder crashed,
and rain started flying every which way

Randy meant to turn back,

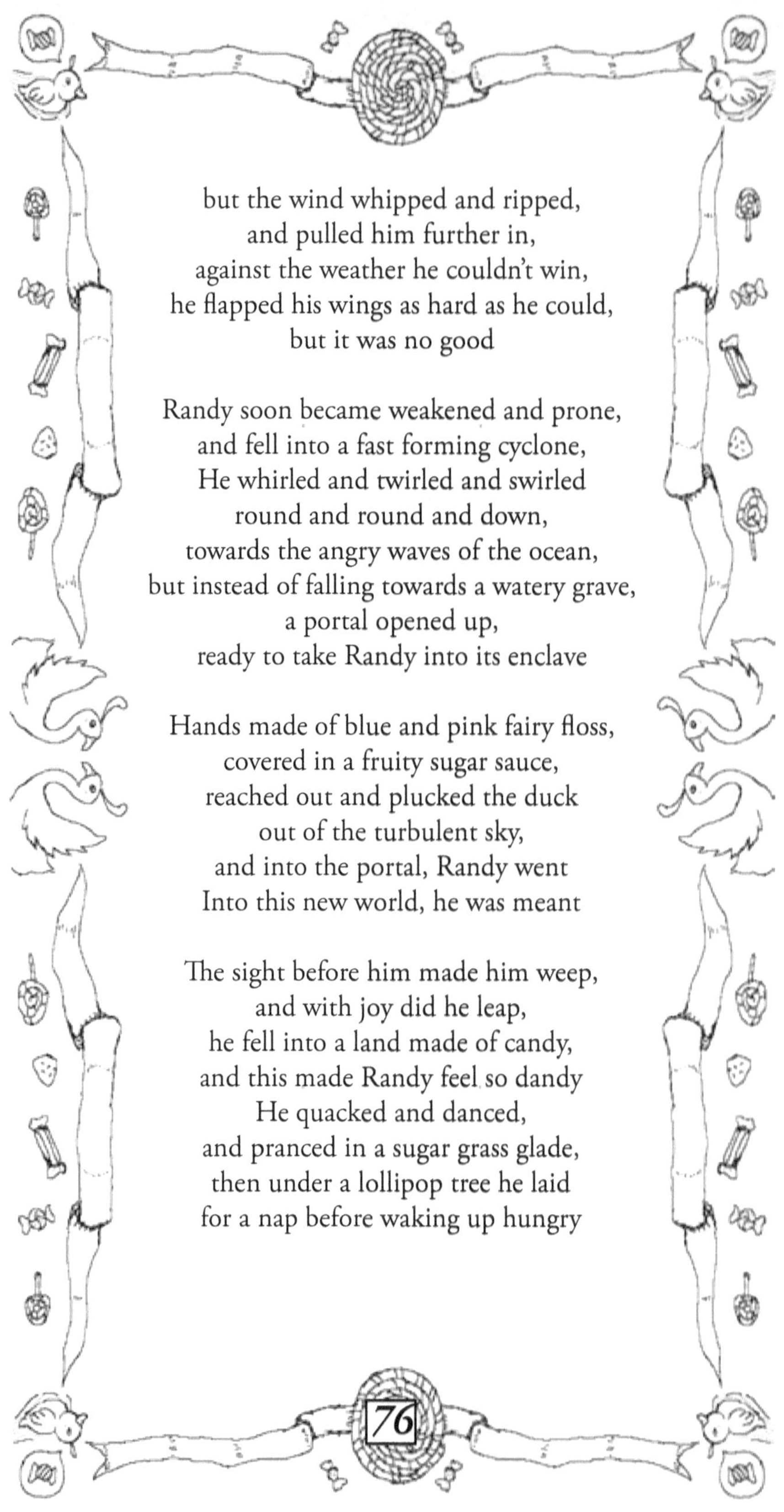

but the wind whipped and ripped,
and pulled him further in,
against the weather he couldn't win,
he flapped his wings as hard as he could,
but it was no good

Randy soon became weakened and prone,
and fell into a fast forming cyclone,
He whirled and twirled and swirled
round and round and down,
towards the angry waves of the ocean,
but instead of falling towards a watery grave,
a portal opened up,
ready to take Randy into its enclave

Hands made of blue and pink fairy floss,
covered in a fruity sugar sauce,
reached out and plucked the duck
out of the turbulent sky,
and into the portal, Randy went
Into this new world, he was meant

The sight before him made him weep,
and with joy did he leap,
he fell into a land made of candy,
and this made Randy feel so dandy
He quacked and danced,
and pranced in a sugar grass glade,
then under a lollipop tree he laid
for a nap before waking up hungry

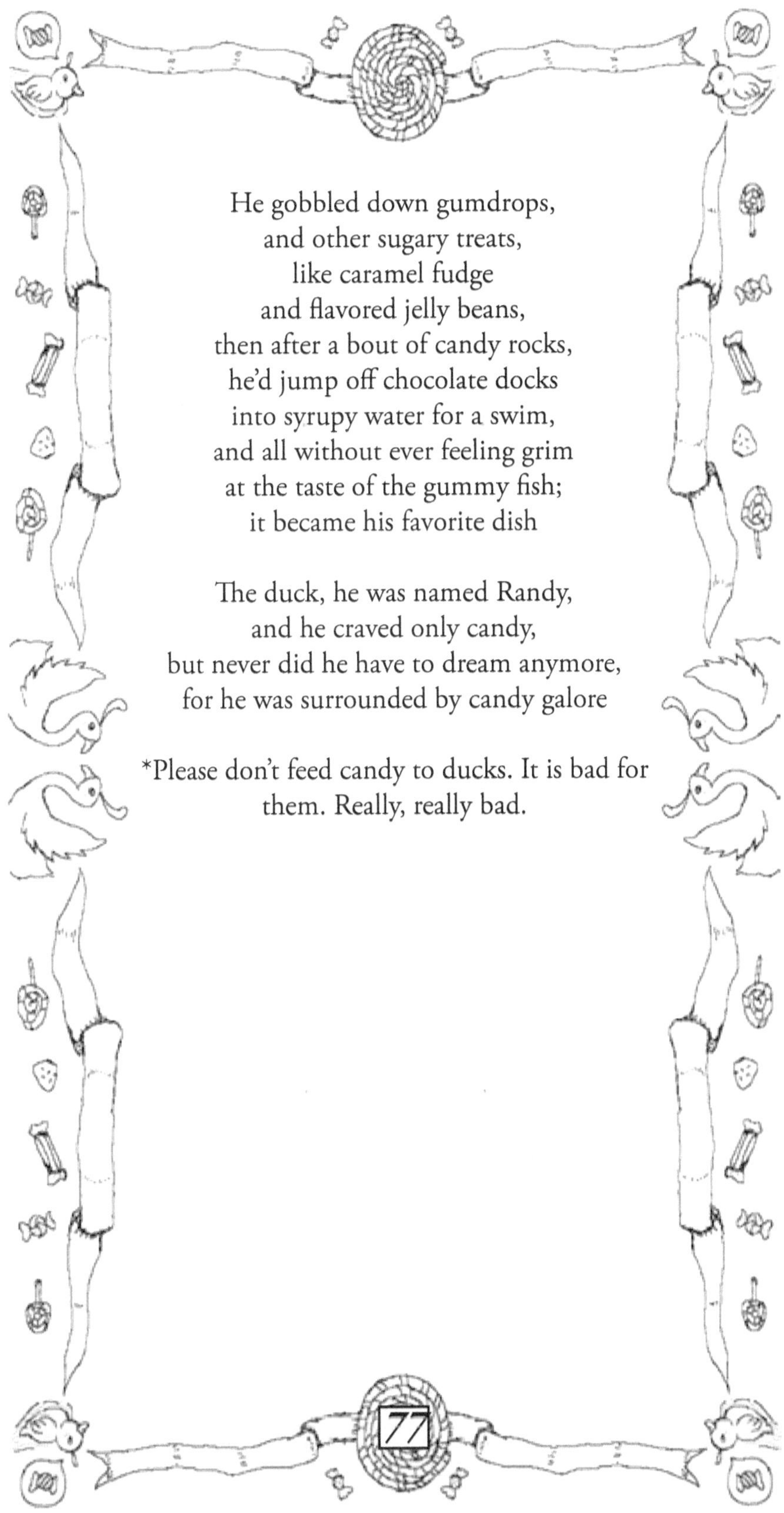

He gobbled down gumdrops,
and other sugary treats,
like caramel fudge
and flavored jelly beans,
then after a bout of candy rocks,
he'd jump off chocolate docks
into syrupy water for a swim,
and all without ever feeling grim
at the taste of the gummy fish;
it became his favorite dish

The duck, he was named Randy,
and he craved only candy,
but never did he have to dream anymore,
for he was surrounded by candy galore

*Please don't feed candy to ducks. It is bad for
them. Really, really bad.

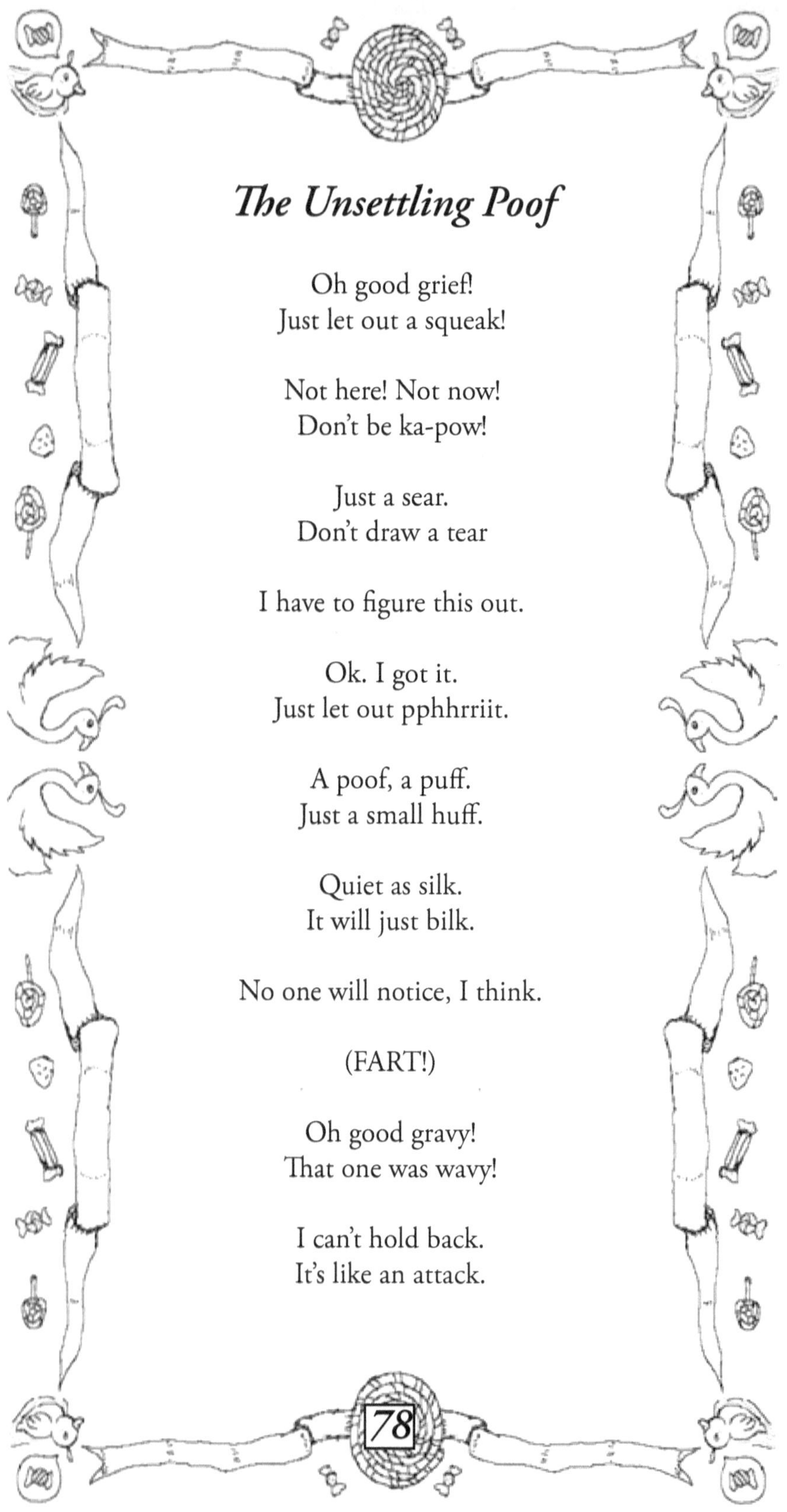

The Unsettling Poof

Oh good grief!
Just let out a squeak!

Not here! Not now!
Don't be ka-pow!

Just a sear.
Don't draw a tear

I have to figure this out.

Ok. I got it.
Just let out pphhrriit.

A poof, a puff.
Just a small huff.

Quiet as silk.
It will just bilk.

No one will notice, I think.

(FART!)

Oh good gravy!
That one was wavy!

I can't hold back.
It's like an attack.

The clutch kicked in.
The wheels they spin.

Not much I can do now.

Sorry folks.
This was not a joke.

But ya gotta admit,
at least it quit.

And this poem can finally stop

Dream Sweet

Dream sweet
no matter where you fly.
Whether your wings are clipped
or just starting to grow,
you'll get there someway; someday
Don't ever deny that you can fly.

If all us little birdies
couldn't have that hope,
then what good would
feathers be for dreamers like
you and me?

Alas, Farewell

And so alas,
we must say our
farewells and our goodnights,
for we have reached the end
of the pages, end of the text,
and so alas, farewell!

But this isn't the final time,
we say goodbye,
you can always come back
for a visit, whether it be for
just a poem or to reread
the whole tome,
your presence is always welcome
within this little book,
but for now,
alas, farewell!

Acknowledgements

We would like to thank Foster Green for putting together the layout of the book. He has a great eye for design! He saved us hours of frustration and troubleshooting. Thank you, my dude!

And thank you to our friends, family, Bikers Against Child Abuse, and our supporters. And an extra special thank you to you for reading our book!

On another note, we are thrilled to be able to re-release our collection. When we first released it, our knowledge of putting a book together was minimal at best. And now, with time and growth, we've been able to learn so much more and put together a better book for all to enjoy.

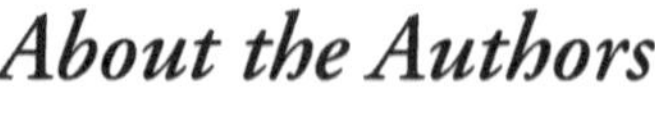

About the Authors
Andrea Standifer

"The Eccentric Blonde" would be the name of the movie if they ever made one about me. Ok, not really, but it is fun to dream. Nope. I enjoy simple pleasures, such as a good fart joke. My cravings include comic books, video games, and pizza. Making someone smile is worth more than gold to me, and singing karioke is my version of a public performance. "Whimsy and Weirdos: Poetry for the Unique" is my third book that I have written, and I could not ask for a better writing partner than "unicorn". to anyone out there who is struggling with their own self worth, it is ok to be yourself. Your weirdness is just your creativity trying to find it's way out into the world.

Poems written by Andrea "Pegasus" Standifer

Let Sleeping Dragons Lie, The Fairy's Last Wish, The Jester Sings, A Mother's Last Stand, The Painted Riverbed, The Horizon Calls, Oath, Deal With It, Screw You, Burn Your Closet, Fighting with Myself, Descend Then Reascend, Her Name Was Amy, Writing for My Sanity, Video Game Query, Spontaneous Word Play,Happy Place, Empty Space, Chocolate!, The Unsettling Poof

Machelle Berglund

I grew up on the wild plains of Southeastern South Dakota. I was often encouraged to pursue my passions and found that I had a knack for writing. I also enjoy painting, drawing, playing video games, and playing Dungeons and Dragons with my friends. I am a proud alum of the Americorps NCCC program. "Whimsy and Weirdos" is the first book I have written, though it won't be the last! It was really fun working on this book with Pegasus! To all the weirdos out there, I hope you find what you seek out there on the journey called life. You only live this life once, and it can change at any moment for the better or the worst. Why not see where it takes you?

Poems written by Machelle "Unicorn" Berglund

A Little Welcoming Poem, Let Us Begin…, A Gathering of Adventurers, Outside the Window, By the Fireside, Princess Misery, In My Garden, Envy the Sky, Gift of Dreams, Drink Down the Stars, If I Could Color You, Sometimes They Forget, To Those of Any Faith, Always Been a Weirdo, A Decision on Doors, As Your Hands Age, Wings, Would if I Could, Go Beyond, Randy the Candy Loving Duck, Dream Sweet, Alas Farewell

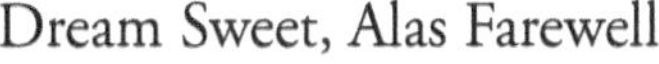